SOUL FOOD

A 40-Day Supply for Busy People

JIM DICK

RIVER
PUBLISHING

River Publishing & Media Ltd
Barham Court
Teston
Maidstone
Kent
ME18 5BZ
United Kingdom

info@river-publishing.co.uk

ISBN 978-1-908393-21-0
Printed in the United Kingdom

Contents

Dedication

To Margery –

A special woman who has been the love of my life for over 50 years – beautiful inside and out and possessing a deep spiritual maturity that has enriched my life and the lives of many others.

About the Author

Jim was born one night in May 1941 while the German Luftwaffe was bombing Clydebank. His father, also Jim, was an engineer in the local steelworks in Motherwell and a Church of Scotland elder. The home was small by modern standards – two rooms (a living room and bedroom), no bathroom but an inside toilet. It was shared by Jim's mother and father, grandparents, 18-year-old brother Tom and his 15-year-old sister Ina, so the addition of a "late-in-life" baby caused some disruption. And there was a war on.

Twelve years later, due to his father's terminal throat cancer, the family became aware of Alex Tee, a fiery young evangelist who was throwing the rather staid religious community in Motherwell into turmoil by his unorthodox evangelistic methods.

Jim came to Christ through the ministry of Duncan Campbell, who had been invited by Alex Tee to come down from the Hebrides to conduct a two-week tent mission in Motherwell. Although he was only 12 at the time, the moment of Jim's conversion was a very powerful and never-to-be-forgotten experience.

While Jim was still in his teens, he became aware of the call of God to the full-time ministry. However, he followed sound advice from Jimmy Salter, a visiting missionary from the Congo revival, to first serve his time in the steel works. Jim did just that and qualified eventually as an engineering draughtsman.

In June of 1963, Jim married Margery Stewart in the Motherwell Elim Church and in September of the same year he went to the Elim Bible College which at that time was located in Clapham, London. He has been a minister with the Elim Pentecostal Church for 45 years.

During his years in full-time ministry he served mainly as a local pastor in Felixstowe, Cardiff, Kingstanding, Bristol and Kilsyth. Jim has also acted as Elim's National Youth Director, Principal of Regents Theological College and Regional Superintendent for the Scottish Region. He has twice been a member of the Elim Executive Council, now known as the National Leadership Team.

Jim and Margery were blessed with three children – Yvonne, Lorraine and Andrew. For 35 years, their life in ministry had all the usual challenges but mainly great happiness in serving God. But at 7:40 on the morning of Tuesday Feb 7, 1998, their life faced a dramatic change.

Their daughter, Lorraine had not long returned from Bangladesh where she had been working with VSO (Voluntary Service Overseas) helping to train nurses. She had been very ill on her return with an e coli-type infection. While Margery visited her, she discovered the real truth behind her emaciated condition: Lorraine was a heroin addict. So began a nightmare journey with their daughter through the twilight world of heroin addiction.

Eventually Jim and Margery discovered that Lorraine had been raped by four policemen in Bangladesh when she had gone into a police station to report the theft of her purse. Lorraine had turned to heroin to blot out the trauma of her sexual violation and the policemen's threats that if she told anyone she would never get out of Bangladesh. Despite all the best efforts of family, friends, and Teen Challenge, Lorraine died from her addiction on November 23, 2004.

Not long after that, Jim and Margery's other daughter, Yvonne, began her own fight with ill health. Following an accident while on holiday, she contacted viral pneumonia and died in a hospital on Gran Canaria, 18 months after the death of her sister.

Throughout this protracted time of pain and grief, Jim and Margery became increasingly aware of the comfort and stability that the word of God brings. They realised the importance of not just a casual reading of favourite passages, but the systematic reading of the whole scriptures. They have sought to understand the whole purpose and plan of God, even in suffering and setbacks, because, "in everything God is at work."

Soul Food is more than a collection of nice thoughts; it is the delivery of lessons learned from 57 years of walking with God in happy times and hard times. It is about getting to know him through his word, which is able to thoroughly equip us for every good work. With the help of the Holy Spirit we are enabled to live life victoriously: not controlled by circumstances or feelings, but comforted and directed by every word that proceeds from the mouth of God.

Foreword

Some manuscripts are written in the clinical isolation of academia or from well-intentioned reflections of the theoretician – not so this book. The pages that you are about to read, and the wisdom you are about to encounter, have been forged on the anvil of reality and distilled in the crucible of a proven faith. In some cases, their perspective has been filtered through the cleansing lens of tears as well as the enriching experience of joy.

An old television advertisement suggested that if small children could create their own menus, their diet would mostly consist of choc ice and chips – fast food that lacked nutritional value. Similarly, there is a superficial kind of "spirituality" that tantalises the taste buds, but fails to strengthen bones and build muscle.

The soul food that Jim Dick places before us is "haute cuisine" indeed. It is free of additives and artificial colouring. The banquet you are about to enjoy is biblically based and spiritually sound.

Jim Dick and I have been friends for over forty years. The two years that we worked alongside one another in the same church were among the richest and most rewarding that I have ever spent, and I cherish their memory. It is impossible to operate closely with someone without being aware of their flaws and inconsistencies – but I have yet to find them in Jim. What I witnessed in his home perfectly paralleled his persona in the pulpit.

This book is long overdue but, like a good meal eagerly anticipated, this soul food will not disappoint. Be prepared to be built up, affirmed, challenged and affirmed. The banquet is ready.

Bon appetit!

John Glass
General Superintendent, Elim Pentecostal Churches

Introduction

My hope is that this book will truly give you food for your soul. No matter how busy we are, our bodies need food or the busyness will soon stop. Our souls are no different. Only the Good Shepherd can restore the soul, but we are responsible for maintaining our soul's health.

This is not a manual to show you how to double your income in six easy steps (or your church for that matter), but healthy food for hungry souls. My purpose is to help open up to the reader the wonderful life wisdom that there is in the Scriptures. The Bible is full of practical wisdom, mined from the lives of real people who faced real-life issues, and preserved for us by the Holy Spirit so that *"through the encouragement of the Scriptures we might have hope."*

The Bible is like a deep mine – there is so much more beneath the surface and with some digging we can access its amazing treasures. I want to help you, the reader, in your own search of the scriptures so that you begin to read with increasing enthusiasm and pleasure.

The days we live in require believers who are robust in their knowledge and walk with God. Some people only want the pleasant bits, the aspects of God that make them feel good with nice comfortable truths. But there is so much more to God – he is not simple and seldom explains himself but wants us to have a faith that can confidently face life.

We need to push through even when things are not going the way we want them to – to develop a level of faith like Job that can say *"though he slay me yet I will hope in him"* (Job 13:15). As the three Hebrew exiles said, *"Even if he does not* [rescue us]*... we will not serve your gods"* (Daniel 3:18). The prophet Daniel declared that *"the people who know their God shall be strong and do exploits"* (Daniel 11:32, KJV). Through the Bible we gain knowledge of God which will give us strength for extraordinary living.

I want to help you discover, or rediscover, the sheer pleasure there is in the unadulterated and straightforward word of God. Christ makes us fit for heaven, but the word and the Spirit makes us fit for earth. Through the Spirit-anointed word, we discover how to live life well and in a God-glorifying way. In his Introduction to Proverbs, Eugene Peterson puts it as "living well, living life in robust sanity."

Let's get back to the wonderful stories, events and characters of scripture. I have not tried to extract every lesson from every story but have left plenty of room for you to draw your own conclusions and also to allow space for the Holy Spirit to make his own unique application. By re-engaging with the Bible stories we discover wisdom for life and a world of surprises.

In Isaiah 64 the prophet's heart is revealed. In the first 5 verses he looks up to God and is overwhelmed. In verses 5-7 he looks out at humanity and is appalled. Then in verses 8 – 12 he looks forward to the future and is reassured.

But in verse three we read, "you did awesome things that we did not expect." God loves to surprise us by doing things we don't expect, awesome things. As you read, may you find the surprisingly wonderful life-wisdom that there is in Bible and discover food for your soul.

You can contact me by email at jimdick41@gmail.com

1

The God Who Surprises

- part one

—⟋⟍—

Everyone loves a surprise. I met an architect in the Philippines who secretly learned to play the flute so that on his wedding day he could surprise his wife by playing for her at the ceremony. She was indeed surprised! Our God is a God of surprises.

My early upbringing in the Church of Scotland conditioned my thinking about God. I perceived him to be intimidating, serious, strict and rather distant. I never associated him with nice surprises.

Jesus came to show us what God is really like, and we get wonderful surprises when we look at his life. The New Testament is full of amazing and delightful things that Jesus did. They give us a wholly different view of God than the sterile, joyless and harsh view often presented by religion and the media.

What a surprise when Jesus healed a blind man by spitting in his eye! And what a surprise when he made a detour into the country of the despised Samaritans to meet an immoral woman – who became one of his greatest witnesses.

I hope this short excursion to Jericho to meet another surprising miracle of Jesus will help you get to know your Saviour better and want to follow him more closely. This is more than just knowing your Bible or theology; it's getting to know our God and Saviour.

Many people want "bits" of Jesus – the bits they like, the Jesus Christ Superstar, the miracle worker, the one who will bless them and make them happy. First century Jews were looking for a Messiah who would deliver them from the occupying Romans and fulfil their dreams for national greatness.

But there is so much more for us to know. The real Jesus is far greater than the Jesus you know at this moment; there are still so many more surprises. He is wonderfully human but awesomely divine.

Luke 19 sets the scene for our surprise – it is the story of a poor little, lonely rich man. Maybe "tea with the tax man" would be an easier title.

Mother Teresa once said, "To those who think they should come out to Calcutta to help in my mission – look around you where you are – there are lepers in your neighbourhood, they are called 'the lonely'." Zacchaeus was a very lonely man. He lived in a busy and prosperous city and no doubt had a good home and lifestyle but because of his despised occupation, he lived a very isolated life.

Sometimes behind the nicest front doors in the smartest neighbourhoods there are some very unhappy and lonely people. I recently came across a website called "Rent-a-friend." For a monthly subscription and a small hourly rate you could rent a friend to be with you for a set amount of time. How sad!

Jesus spent a disproportionate amount of time with people who were outside the circle of "decent" society, people who did not fit in with the religious establishment. He had a special interest in people who had doubts and questions. He loved a challenge – people who had messed up their lives and were wondering how to get back to God.

A lot of people called Jesus their friend that others would not want to be seen with – a prostitute, a shady business man, a confused religious leader. He wasn't interested in enhancing his reputation and was never afraid to challenge religious and cultural taboos to enable him to connect with people. So when he visited Jericho he connected with the two most unlikely people in the city – Zacchaeus and Bartimaeus. Zach and Bart, the banker and the beggar.

It was a surprise that Jesus ever went to Jericho in the first place. It was a place that was under a curse (Joshua 6:26) but he went and turned it into a place of blessing for at least two people.

He also chose a surprising place to meet with Zach. Jesus did not wait for Zacchaeus to make an appointment to see him – he sought out this deeply despised man in a tree and extended a hand of friendship. There was no formal conversation, simply a request to come to his home for a meal. And what a life-changing meal that turned out to be!

2

The God Who Surprises

- part two

—⁓—

Zacchaeus was the chief tax collector in Jericho and had become wealthy collecting taxes from his own people for the Romans. This occupation certainly did not endear him to the Jews. The tax collectors of the day were not afraid to add their own "cut" on top of the Roman demand. I used to go and speak at a Christian Union in my local tax office; they referred to themselves as "the saints in squeezer's household"!

Despite his wealth, Zacchaeus knew he was empty inside and that his wealth did not buy peace of mind. He had heard the stories that were circulating about Jesus – that he was not afraid to meet with undesirables like himself. Being a short man he thought he could get a better view of Jesus by situating himself in a nearby tree. Little did he know that Jesus had determined that he would meet with Zach on this visit and at the very tree he had climbed? I read that after 9/11 there was a lot of controversy over the sharing out of the millions of dollars collected for the families of the victims. On the day of the disaster, investment bankers were running down the stairs of the Twin Towers to escape the flames, while firemen were running up the stairs to rescue people. Yet the families of the investment bankers were offered considerably more money than the families of the firemen who died in the tragedy.

Apparently the life of an investment banker was considered to be worth more than that of a fireman. Yet the cross of Christ reveals the value that God places on the worth of every individual regardless of their position in life. When others looked at Zacchaeus they saw someone of no value, but when Jesus looked at him he saw a man worth saving.

Jesus went into Jericho to meet two people – the poorest man and the richest man. Both needed him. Luke 19:10 is one of the great "purpose" verses in the New Testament: *"For the Son of Man came to seek and save what was lost."* Jesus came not just to save the lost but to seek and to save the lost. He did not just wait for Zach to come looking for him; he went looking for this hurting man.

There are many marginalised groups in society and Christians do not always have a good record of coping with those who think differently than us. What a challenge to adopt Jesus' attitude towards marginalised groups and go out of our way to meet them. Jesus never went soft on sin, but he did show abundant love and grace to those who were hungry to discover the life he offered.

When Zacchaeus looked down into the face of Jesus, he was looking into the face of pure love. He had looked into the faces of condemnation but now he met compassion. He had met the law, but now he met grace.

I try to imagine that face, the face of the most alive man who ever lived. The glory of God was in the face of Jesus! Zacchaeus had shivered in the cold climate of religious condemnation, now he basked in the sunshine of amazing grace. Jesus did not invite him to a lecture in the local synagogue, based on the text, *"You shall not steal."*

Instead, he invited himself to the man's house for a meal, saying, *"I must stay at your house today."*

Zacchaeus must have been surprised that Jesus knew his name. The world population is fast approaching 7 billion, yet God knows the name of everyone and every detail of their lives. He calls the countless stars by name and when a sparrow falls, he knows which one is missing. He is an awesome God acquainted with every tiny detail about his creation.

But now we are in for another surprise in this story and that is the amazing sermon that changed this man. No words are recorded to have been spoken and yet it brought about a remarkable response which left Zacchaeus financially poorer but spiritually richer.

Francis of Assisi said: "Preach Christ at all times, and if necessary use words." The Holy Spirit was at work awakening faith in Zach's heart, showing him what he needed to repent of and make restitution for. By the end of the visit, salvation had come to the man and his family. It affected his finances and would change the way he did business for the rest of his life.

It is pure speculation, but I wonder whether Zacchaeus and Bartimaeus became friends after Jesus left?

I like to think so; after all, both had their lives radically changed by the same man. Maybe the two became founder members of the first New Testament Church of Jericho? Despite being from diametrically opposite positions in society, they both had life-changing experiences when they met Christ.

Our God loves to surprise us: *"You did awesome things that we did not expect."*

I hope you will still be on the lookout for some of God's surprises in your life today. If you are interested in a postscript blessing, read Psalm 139.

3
Sister Act

- part one

—ɯ—

This is the story of five sisters whose bold action not only affected life for them and the women of their generation but also for generations to come. We know of the determined action of women like Emmeline Pankhurst and other suffragettes to obtain rights for women; this is a similar story predating them by thousands of years.

There is a bravery that does not arise in a moment of crisis, but is chosen before the event and entered into in a cool, deliberate way. Every day many disabled people get up and face a predictable day with life-challenging obstacles and difficulties with determination. They may not get a Victoria Cross, but show courage of a very high order. It is not energised by the adrenalin of the moment but often finds its source in a daily supply of God's grace. True grit!

You may not be called upon to rush into a burning building to rescue a person in danger but, nevertheless, you can exhibit the quiet courage of facing every day consistently and dependably, doing your job to the best of your ability, supporting your family, paying your taxes, being a good neighbour, helping in the community and participating in your local church.

I watched a documentary recently on Indonesian workers who daily walk into the mouth of an active volcano to gather sulphur. This entails breathing toxic fumes which severely affect their lungs. They carry baskets on their shoulders which can be twice their body weight and each man earns the princely sum of $5 per load. They repeat this dangerous occupation every day so that they can provide for their wives and children. Now that is a high degree of courage.

This Bible story from the book of Numbers introduces us to five sisters called Mahlah, Noah, Hoglah, Milcah, and Tirzah; none of which are in today's top ten popular names!

They lived in times of momentous change. The nation of Israel, because of unbelief, had endured forty years of life in a barren wilderness but now a new generation was getting ready to enter the Promised Land. In preparation, Moses had initiated a second census of the whole nation to determine who would be eligible for an inheritance – a mammoth but essential task as it would save inter-tribal disputes later.

As they worked through a list of more than 600,000 men, they came to the family of a deceased man called Zelophehad. Unfortunately he had died without his wife giving birth to a son but he was survived by five daughters, so it was assumed that his inheritance could not be passed on.

That's when the unthinkable happened. Bear in mind that this was not a local gathering of some neighbours convened at the end of their row of tents. This was an august meeting of the whole nation complete with top officials – Moses, Aaron, Joshua, Caleb, the seventy elders and the tribal heads, as well as every man above the age of twenty.

Suddenly there was a disturbance among the mass of people and five very nervous young ladies pushed their way to the front of the crowd. They stood in front of Moses with an unthinkable request: *"Why should our father's name disappear from his clan because he had no son? Give us property among our father's relatives"* (Numbers 27:4).

Stunned silence – nothing like this had ever been done before! This was bold and startling and it left Moses so nonplussed that he immediately called for a recess to give him time to talk to God about these "disturbers of the peace."

These girls must have been thinking about this for some time and planned their action aware of the possible repercussions; after all, this was very much a male-oriented society. A positive and far-reaching revolution had been brewing in the cooking tent of the Zelophehad family.

It's not just the powerful personalities and the big names that can make a difference in society. It's possible you have never heard of these five sisters, yet the bold action of these hitherto unknown girls has affected property rights for Jewish women ever since.

The Bible is full of remarkable deeds often done by quite unremarkable people.

These girls were not prepared to just be spectators of big events; they had the courage to shape some of those events. It's easy to conform but much more effective to transform.

Noah, Hoglah, Tirzah, Milcah and Mahlah, the first suffragettes, have long since passed to their graves, but I believe there are some life-lessons for us in the 21st century.

They had vision

Vision comes from faith and faith comes from hearing. I imagine these girls sitting round the campfires with other Israelite young people, listening to the stories Joshua and Caleb told of the Promised Land. After all, they had actually been there and tasted the fruit. As the sisters listened, something began to be ignited in their hearts.

What they had already enjoyed for their short lives was good, even remarkable — the daily supply of manna, the miracle food from heaven, plus a copious water supply for the whole nation from a rock that always seemed to be there. Then there was the guidance, light, warmth and shade from the cloud and pillar of fire in the centre of the camp. Added to that, they experienced clothes and footwear that did not wear out for forty years, as well as feet that never swelled with desert travel.

Yes, they had already seen some quite amazing things, but what they heard sparked a desire for more from Jehovah. It is so easy in our personal lives and church life to settle for the good and miss the best. In the midst of nation-shaping events with prominent players, five hitherto unknown young ladies were catching a vision to have a part in the nation's greatest venture — the Promised Land.

4

Sister Act

- part two

—⟋⟍—

The action of the five sisters was audacious and must have left the male-only gathering gasping with astonishment. Culture has been described as "the way we do things around here," and five girls asking for property was not how things were done around there. The usual way was for girls to get married and share in what their husbands had. These girls obviously did not believe in settling for the status quo – they had a bold vision of something better.

The Kingdom of God is overcrowded with settlers; we are desperately in need of more pioneers who believe in the Star Trek slogan – to boldly go. There are still many challenges in 21st century Britain and abroad that will demand the spirit and courage of a modern-day Wilberforce, Raikes, Muller or Booth. It's not always the dramatic action that makes the headlines; these girls just asked a question – "Why can't we inherit our father's property?"

It has been often said – "If you want to see what you've never seen before, then be prepared to do what you've never done before." These girls certainly did something that had never been done before.

We have looked at the faith and vision that motivated their courage but let's consider three more life-lessons for 21st century believers:

The five sisters were united

Divided they probably would not have succeeded, but together they were able to face the challenge. When my wife and I fought a seven-year battle with our daughter's heroin addiction, we were enormously grateful for the support of caring people. The members of our church in Kilsyth walked with us through that dark valley, and there were times when it was their support that kept us going.

The Apostle Paul was an incredibly strong man, yet he surrounded himself with great people, male and female. You only have to look at Romans 16 to be amazed at the number and variety of helpers who enhanced his life and ministry. The small number of people you spend most of your free time with will affect your life more than you realise.

Leviticus 26:8 has an impossible calculation – *"Five of you will chase a hundred, and a hundred of you will chase ten thousand."* Great is the power of synergy. These girls caught a vision for something bigger and better, but they also supported each other in the fostering and fulfilling of that vision.

The five sisters had a good attitude

Once they were convinced of the challenge they were going to make, they had a choice to make as to how they would do it. They were not hatching a rebellion among the cooking pots. They chose not to start a protest movement campaigning for women's rights, marching round the camp with banners or even chaining themselves to the tent poles of the Tabernacle. The sisters were radicals but not rebels.

God will not bless those with a rebellious spirit; he is not only interested in what you are doing but also how and why you are doing it. Their choice was to respectfully present their case in the right manner to the right people. It is possible to cancel out the effect of doing the right thing by doing it in the wrong way and for the wrong reason.

Jesus exhibited this right submissive attitude at age twelve in Jerusalem. Despite knowing who his real Father was, he chose to go down to Nazareth and be subject to his parents and their way of life for the next eighteen years until it was God's time.

After the sisters' bombshell, Moses retired to his "tent of meeting" to talk to God and the answer he got seemed to indicate an enthusiastic response – *"what Zelophehad's daughters are saying is right, you must certainly give them property"* (Numbers 27:7).

Jehovah said yes! What a shock to the girls, to Moses, to the leaders, to all the men. The accepted customs of the day were being changed; the future for the generations who would follow was being rewritten because Moses enshrined it in national law.

Sin has robbed women of so much of the dignity of equality but this event was a start along the road that would culminate in the restoration ministry of Christ. In the first century AD, Paul would write that *"There is neither Jew nor Gentile, neither slave nor free, nor is there male and female, for you are all one in Christ Jesus"* (Galatians 3:28). The girls had exercised visionary faith and God is pleased with faith.

The friends of the five sisters could have said "it's never been done, it can't be done"; others would say that they were too young, the wrong gender or "you can't fight culture." But they proved them all wrong because they had faith mixed with courage and a willingness to take a risk.

There is just one more lesson for us from these remarkable girls:

The five sisters had perseverance

Moses had given them a promise but they had to wait quite a few years for its fulfilment – there was warfare and the nation had to wait to see the land finally become theirs. But the day did come and the five sisters – Noah, Hoglah, Milcah, Mahlah and Tirzah finally stood on their own inheritance and inherited their piece of the Promised Land.

I hope the action of these sisters has challenged you to ask God to give you a fresh vision and the courage to see it through. It may require you to change some things in your lifestyle and your allocation of time, energy and resources to become more fully involved and committed to God's Kingdom.

If you want to read this surprising story for yourself, then go to Numbers chapter 27, Joshua chapter 17:3-6 and Numbers chapter 36.

5

From Survival to Revival

- part one

—⁂—

I have only ever been in two really bad storms at sea and on both occasions I was sea-sick. When I was a teenager, a large Pentecostal church in Scotland hired a paddle steamer, the Jeanie Deans, for a day's sailing on the West Coast. It started well with hundreds of Christian passengers in good heart and voice as we sailed down the Clyde but when the ship hit a dreadful storm in open water it was not a pretty sight.

They say that sea-sickness has two stages; the first is when you're afraid you will die, and the second is when you're afraid you won't die!

In Acts chapter 27, Paul was in one of the greatest storms of his life. Paul was a master strategist in mission work, establishing churches in strategic cities, gathering converts, teaching and training them, appointing elders and commissioning them to evangelise their district and region. Through this, the gospel was impacting the whole Roman Empire.

But Paul had one big ambition – *"I must visit Rome"* (Acts 19:21). This was not the demand of a tourist with another city to tick off his "must-see" list – it was the desire of an apostle who wanted to take the message of Christ into the heart of the empire.

Eventually in Acts 27 Paul was on his way to Rome, but perhaps not the way he had expected, as he was in chains and escorted by soldiers as a prisoner to appear before Caesar. Little did Caesar realize whose fare he was paying to come to Rome!

So, in Acts 27 we find Paul, on his way to Rome, fulfilling his long-held ambition to get to that city when suddenly they were hit by a life-threatening storm. *"We finally gave up all hope of being saved"* (Acts 27:20) summed up the fear of all two hundred and seventy six people on board the doomed vessel.

Many thoughts must have gone through Paul's mind at this time. Perhaps he was wondering, "Why is God allowing this to happen to me when I am on course for the greatest opportunity for the gospel – preaching in Rome and perhaps in front of Caesar?" Or maybe he was remembering how Jesus once rescued Peter by walking to him on the water and speaking a word to silence the storm. Would Jesus save him in such a dramatic way?

Storms are not always a good indicator of whether or not you are in or out of the will of God. Jonah was in a storm out of the will of God, and here was Paul in the will of God but also in a storm. Storms come to all of us.

An angel messenger

At this point in the story there is a very dramatic divine intervention – God sent an angel to tell Paul not to be afraid as he was going to make it to Rome. Paul was afraid but I am sure it was not of dying in the storm, as he had faced death on many occasions. I think the fear would be of not accomplishing God's great purpose in reaching into the heart of the Roman Empire.

The angel gave Paul a message for himself, *"Do not be afraid,*

Paul, you must stand trial before Caesar," and then there was a bonus message for the other passengers – *"God has graciously given you the lives of all who sail with you"* (Acts 27:24).

There is wisdom for us all here – Paul had received a very clear message that he and the other passengers were all going to be safe. Yet the circumstances did not immediately change; in fact they got worse, and there appear to have been several more days of nail-biting anxiety still to go, including the total loss of the ship and the trauma of a shipwreck.

Receiving a powerful and precise promise from God does not mean that circumstances are necessarily going to change quickly. In the absence of an immediate rescue, Paul still made the choice to believe the promise.

Faith is *"being sure of what we hope for and certain of what we do not see."* This confidence in the certainty of God's promise allowed Paul to stand up in front of the other passengers and declare, *"I have faith in God that it will happen just as he told me."*

The fulfilment of every promise has its own process and timing. We don't have control over that, but we can choose to hold on to the promise despite unchanged circumstances.

"Nevertheless" (verse 26) is the bit in between the promise and the fulfilment. Unfortunately it is the gap that too many fall into when their impatience gets the better of them. The gap between a promise and its fulfilment is like the gap between sowing and reaping.

6

From Survival to Revival

- part two

—⁓—

Many years ago I heard John Shelbourne, a prominent Assemblies of God minister, speak on this story from Acts 27, and it left a lasting impression on my life. The apostle Paul received a wonderful promise of deliverance from the storm but it seems that the fulfilment was still in the pending tray. The storm was still raging; in fact the circumstances got worse, but Paul was holding on to his confidence in God that everyone was going to be delivered.

If you fast forward the story to Acts chapter 28, you will see what amazing surprises God had in store for the travellers. They did not yet know that they were going to be shipwrecked on the island of Malta, but when the time arrived for their miracle deliverance there would be:

- Unusual kindness from the islanders
- Warmth and a welcome

- Miraculous preservation for Paul when he was bitten by a viper
- Amazing hospitality from the chief official of the island
- Miracles and opportunities for evangelism
- All the sick on the island would be healed
- Abundant provision for their onward voyage

Malta had never seen anything like this before and has never seen anything like it since.

This is what lay ahead for them on the other side of God's promise of deliverance but back in the storm they struggled for survival. What Paul did have was a word from God and courage to believe and declare it, but the rest of the passengers were just desperately trying to stay alive in a dreadful storm.

21st Century Church

Today's western church is in a survival-threatening storm, but it's often in storms that our priorities get readjusted. The world now regards the church as an irrelevance and pressure groups like the new atheists are working hard to strip it of all influence in society. For decades there has been a steady decline in overall numbers, a preoccupation with internal issues and church politics, immorality, and a lack of God-centred purpose. Too many churches are working hard to just stay afloat.

However, there are signs that this situation is beginning to change. Recent riots in the UK, a collapsing financial market and accelerating global uncertainty are combining to awaken a desire within many people to rediscover God. These are significant days for the UK and the western church – a season of challenge and change that must not be missed.

This story contains some important lessons for the church today. I will introduce them and leave plenty of space for you, the reader, to draw relevant conclusions.

While Paul was still hanging onto his promise of deliverance, some practical things contributed to changing the situation.

Otherwise they could have just tried to ride out the storm and ended up with a lost opportunity, missed destiny and early death for all on board. Revival is from the Lord, but there are things that we must do to help prepare the way for God to do his sovereign work.

Stop trying to hold together something God is breaking up

The sailors were putting ropes under the ship to try and hold it together, though God had declared it was going to be lost (verse 22). The ship had probably been well designed and built and had served its purpose well but it could no longer handle the situation it was facing. It had been sufficient in the past, but could not copy with the present situation.

Church as we know and practice it may have served well in the past but it is not coping with the demands and opportunities of today. Many believe we are in the second reformation – Luther's first reformation was about what the church believed, but this one is about church practice, how we do church.

We should honour the past and learn from it, but we cannot be controlled by it. Old wineskins are not fit for the fermentation of the new wine that God is producing now. Old mindsets and inflexible methods will not cope with the challenges of engaging with the complexity of multiple cultures.

We cannot be restricted to what happens on a Sunday or what happens within a building we call "church," nor will a hierarchical structure facilitate releasing the whole body of Christ for ministry. Freshness, flexibility and spontaneity are required, not the ropes of tired, worn-out structures.

7
From Survival to Revival

- part three

—ɯ—

Paul and the people on board the stricken vessel did some practical things to help facilitate the miracle deliverance God had promised, as well as the amazing move of God on the island of Malta. They understood the foolishness of trying to hold together something God was going to break up. Now a few more practical steps had to be taken:

The cargo was thrown overboard – Acts 27:18

The cargo represented the commercial enterprise, the profit from this trip. It may have been the owner's future pension or his children's college fees, but what had been all important before the storm was of little value now. Storms do indeed change our priorities, especially in relation to the importance of money.

Holding onto the cargo would be dangerous; it was safer to let it go. Jesus personified money as the god Mammon, which must not be a rival to the true God. We all need money, but it must be kept in its right place as a servant and not a master. If we devote ourselves to it, we can end up being devoured by it.

Giving is not something God just does, it is who God is. God is the greatest giver and everything God is allowed to control, gives. 2 Corinthians 8:1-9 is well worth a read on the grace of giving.

The ship's tackle was discarded – Acts 27:19

The ship's tackle was the machinery for doing the business of sailing, but since it was no longer working it had to go overboard. We have developed very complicated "machinery" for the running of church – committees, programmes, constitutions, books and denominational rules. But in today's challenges, so much of the old machinery is redundant.

Nevertheless, not everything old is bad and not everything new is good. Jesus said,

"Therefore every teacher of the law who has become a disciple in the kingdom of heaven is like the owner of a house who brings out of his storeroom new treasures as well as old." (Matthew 13:52)

The life-boat was cut away – Acts 27:32

Some of the crew wanted to jump ship and under pretext of lowering more anchors, determined to get into the life-boat and make their own way to land. Paul told the centurion to cut it adrift, and he did – a very brave thing to do.

Some Christians feel they have the right to jump ship when things don't please them, and get into their personal life-boat (little fellowships) with people who think as they do. Too many think that church is there to serve them. They will attend, pay their tithes and serve as long as things are going the way they agree with, but when they are not, many hear fictitious calls from God to "move on."

Our churches would be so much stronger if this particular life-boat was permanently cut away. It needs to be replaced with a commitment to continue building together in the hard times as well as easy times. Believers need to grow up and develop a kingdom mentality, dealing with issues biblically instead of jumping into a life-boat and escaping them. The church has the greatest message and the biggest mission, and it will take a united church to see it completed.

The anchors were cut – Acts 27:40

The crew had lowered four anchors from the stern fearing they would be blown onto the rocks; their purpose was to stop them moving on any further. That's what anchors are intended to do, but if these anchors had not been cut away they would never have reached their God-prepared place.

It's amazing how many anchors Christians have developed to keep them safely in one place. These well-used anchors have names like fear, tradition, pride, complacency, laziness, unresolved issues, and unforgiveness. It takes courage to confront them and cut them away, but that's the only way to progress into what God has planned.

The rudder was untied – Acts 27:40

The rudder determines direction and for the travellers to reach their destination, it had to be untied. When we find something good, we tend to set it in stone and fight to keep it that way for ever. They could not hoist a sail and commit to the wind that would blow them into God's prepared place until they untied the rudder.

As well as these practical things to assist progress, they also took time in the midst of the tension to break bread and be refreshed. Then it was time to hoist the sail and commit themselves to the wind which would blow them into God's place. And they made it, all two hundred and seventy six of them, just as God had promised.

The church has received many wonderful promises from God, but we can't just sit back and wait for them to happen. We were never destined to live in survival mode.

There are many "Malta" opportunities waiting for those who are willing to cut the anchors that are stopping them from moving on. Some need to get rid of a life-boat mentality. Sometimes we need to hoist a sail to catch a fresh wind of the Spirit or let go of worn-out procedures. But whatever it takes, revival is a lot better than survival.

8

From a Dirge to a Dance

- part one

—⚏—

Once on a trip to Africa, I was staying in a safari lodge. Early one morning I decided to have a swim in the open-air pool before breakfast. I dived in and while under the water I opened my eyes and to my horror below me I saw a crocodile. Adrenalin and fear kicked in and I think I broke some world speed records in getting out of the pool, expecting at any moment to feel the snapping jaws of the fearsome predator.

I got out and stood on the side of the pool trembling and dripping and had a look at the beast, but to my embarrassment I discovered it was a very well-made mosaic! Things were not as they appeared, and my fears turned out to be groundless.

The book we are going to look at for a few chapters introduces us to a prophet who was in deep depression as he looked at the situation around him. He was making wrong conclusions because he was not in possession of all the facts.

Things were not as they appeared, as he found out.

The book is Habakkuk.

Habakkuk differs from other prophetic books of the Old Testament, which are usually the record of a message from God to the people of God via the prophet of God. Habakkuk is more like a private journal, recording the prophet's struggle as he tried to understand the ways of God.

The book deals with tough questions, and challenges our view of God. We are inclined to change the Westminster Confession from, "Man's chief aim is to glorify God" to "God's chief aim is to satisfy man." There are times when God's ways seem light years beyond ours.

There are three chapters in the book. To help you get a picture of Habakkuk's journey and the vital life lessons we can gain from it, I have given each of the three chapters a title. They record his progress from a dirge to a dance.

From a quick glance at the start of the book and the end it is easy to see a huge difference in the prophet's mood. At the start he is in deep despair, but at the end, even although the circumstances had not changed, the prophet certainly had. You will find him singing, calling on the choir and the orchestra to join him in praise and declaring that his feet felt like hind's feet skipping on the mountain.

What brought about such a dramatic change in this man? Hopefully it will become clear as you progress through the three chapters, with their respective themes of problems, patience, and praise.

Chapter 1 – The prophet's problems

Things were happening in Habakkuk's days that were seriously alarming him. The international situation was dire – the world was in panic, there was instability and insecurity, and great and powerful nations were collapsing. A new player (Babylon) was rising in dominance with nothing seeming able to stop the onward march of this ruthless, fearless and callous threat.

The national situation was no better – Israel, the people of God were seriously backslidden. For a long time God had been warning them through prophets, famines, and calamities but they had not listened. Now judgment was unavoidable and imminent.

Habakkuk described the spiritual condition of the people of God, with words like *"violence, injustice, wrong, destruction, strife and conflict."* The resulting chaos was that *"the law was paralysed, justice was perverted and never prevailed."* When the world most needed a holy and righteous people to lead it through an international crisis, God's people were at their weakest.

It doesn't take a lot of effort to draw a parallel between Habakkuk's day and ours. Serious international changes are taking place, with the power of existing leader nations diminishing and new ones rising in dominance and control. Alongside that is the tragedy of an impotent church, regarded by the world as irrelevant.

But there was another dimension to Habakkuk's problem: in the midst of international and national problems, he was going through his own spiritual crisis. Chapter 1 is a very honest account of Habakkuk's struggle with the dilemma of an apparently absent God when he is most needed. There are two main complaints in chapter 1 that the prophet struggled with – the first, that God was silent and the second, that God appeared inconsistent.

Habakkuk was about to go through a serious and steep learning curve in his knowledge and experience of God.

The prophet's first complaint

"How long, O Lord, must I call for help but you do not listen? Or cry out to you, 'Violence!' but you do not save?" (Habakkuk 1:2)

"Cry out" means to shout out with a disturbed heart, or to scream or yell at the top of one's voice. The prophet is obviously very passionate about this complaint. "Violence" can also be read as "I've been wronged." Perhaps the prophet had a personal matter of justice that God appeared silent on as well.

In the face of blatant injustice when the law of God was being trampled underfoot, when leaders and the rich were violating the rights and the needs of the poor, when official business was often done with bribes – how could God remain distant and silent? This was Habakkuk's complaint, which made him call out to God with passionate prayer.

9
From a Dirge to a Dance

- part two

—∿—

Despite his impassioned prayer, Habakkuk was struggling with a national and international situation that desperately needed God's intervention. He was not the first or the last to go through the hard discipline of a silent heaven. Asaph in Psalm 77 went through a similar experience: *"Will God never show his favour again? Has his unfailing love vanished forever? Has God forgotten to be merciful?"*

In seasons of silence the mature saint learns the importance of walking by faith, not by feeling. Mother Teresa, called the "Mother of the Poor," one of the most recognised figures on the planet, worked in the slums of Calcutta for over half a century. Despite her amazing achievements, she battled with spiritual depression – consistently trying and failing to feel the presence of God. Yet her personal battles did not stop her working for God.

After the silence, Habakkuk finally heard from God, but instead of easing his spiritual burden, this only increased it. In Chapter 1, verse 5, God informed Habakkuk that he was at work, even although Habakkuk was not aware of it –

"Look at the nations and watch – and be utterly amazed (be astounded), for I am doing something in your days that you would not believe even if you were told."

Then God drops the bombshell, and if Habakkuk had a problem before, he had a bigger one now. Although chapter 1 can be heavy, grasping it is vital to appreciating the power of the prophet's breakthrough. Tony Campolo tells of the black preacher who was speaking on the death and resurrection of Christ and throughout the message said, "It's Friday, but Sunday's coming!" Well, it's chapter 1, but chapter 3 is coming!

God declared that he had raised up the Babylonians and was (temporarily) allowing their march of conquest. To further emphasise the fact, God gives a very graphic description of what they were like:

"...that ruthless and impetuous people, who sweep across the whole earth to seize dwellings not their own. They are a feared and dreaded people; they are a law to themselves ... They fly like an eagle swooping to devour; they all come intent on violence ... They mock at kings and scoff at rulers."

They had the ferocity of wolves, the speed of leopards and were as greedy as vultures. The Babylonians were so proud and confident of their military might that it had become their god – *"whose own strength is their god"* (verse 11).

Habakkuk's first complaint was that God was not listening, but his second complaint (beginning at verse 12) was that God's answer appeared inconsistent with his holy character. How could a holy God use such an unholy nation? God's silence was hard but this new revelation was harder. There seems to be a note of incredulity in Habakkuk – *"You, Lord, have appointed them to execute judgment."*

The prophet was stunned – this was challenging his theology that declared, *"Your eyes are too pure to look on evil; you cannot tolerate wrong."* Verses 12 – 16 record his confusion.

God is not consistent by our measurements, nor is he always fair by our standards. Habakkuk wanted a powerful revival in the people of God and swift judgment on the wicked Babylonians, yet what he was hearing was far removed from that. God is God, and he is not required to do things in line with our nice, neat expectations.

R T Kendall wrote a book, *Out of the Comfort Zone*, with the subtitle, "Is your God too nice?" The book has strong but needed teaching for today's "comfort zone" Christians.

The closing question – verse 17

Habakkuk closes chapter 1 with a question – *"Is he (the Babylonian army) to keep on emptying his net, destroying nations without mercy?"*

So what will Habakkuk do in the light of this perplexing revelation? God had been silent when needed most, but his God's revelation of what was happening causes the prophet to be even more confused. At this point many walk away from faith, shaking their heads at the difficulties of pursuing the sometimes hard-to-understand ways of God.

What is your most important possession? Your iPad, your car, your career, your family and friends, health and fitness or perhaps a hobby? The fact is that a Christian's greatest possession is their faith. When Jesus prayed for Peter as he was about to enter the biggest test of his life, it was that his faith would not fail.

Habakkuk's faith was being stretched, not only by the national and international crises but by God's way of working, which was unlike anything he had experienced before. We know from the end of the book that his faith not only survived, but actually grew. He broke through to a confidence in God that rejoices extravagantly, despite the fact that absolutely nothing had changed in his circumstances. The prophet was the one that had changed.

I am so glad that Habakkuk recorded his spiritual journey. It provides 21st century Christians with much-needed wisdom for living in today's complicated world.

10

From a Dirge to a Dance

- part three

—⟪—

Chapter 2 of Habakkuk is the preparation for the breakthrough of chapter 3. For Pentecostals, the second chapter of Acts is exciting and powerful, but the first chapter of Acts, though less dramatic, is the preparation that makes chapter 2 possible. Likewise Habakkuk 2 is the doorway to chapter 3.

Habakkuk chapter 2 – Patience

After the final question of Habakkuk 1, the prophet made a life-affecting choice – he took himself to a lonely place, which happened to be up on one of the city watchtowers, and quietened himself to wait on God: *"I will stand, I will station myself, I will look to see what he will say to me."*

He positioned himself to hear from God. That required patience to wait, which would mean laying aside other things, even legitimate things. He also got himself ready to respond if rebuked by God. It is easier to work than wait, to talk than listen. He closed his mouth, opened his eyes and his ears and waited in expectation for God to speak. And God did.

How long did Habakkuk wait? We don't know. I'm sure his commitment to wait would be tested but it was also rewarded, for in verse 2 God spoke. The prophet was commanded to write down the revelation he was about to get in response to his question, *"are the Babylonians to keep on destroying nations without mercy?"*

The revelation was meant to be preserved for posterity, and had to be written on a stone tablet. It was written to inspire, as a herald was meant to run with it. It would also give reassurance because it looked forward with confidence to the future. Even though there would be a delay, it would not prove false.

The revelation would give the righteous a foundation for unshakable confidence during the coming turbulence, so that *"the righteous could live [and keep on living] by faith."* Faith is the unshakable confidence in God so that no matter how dark the day or difficult the circumstances, there is no doubt as to the final outcome. *"Faith comes from hearing the message"* (Romans 10:17) and as Habakkuk heard the word of the Lord, his faith rose to a crescendo of praise.

So what was the revelation that Habakkuk got about the continuation of the Babylonian tsunami of violence that was sweeping unhindered throughout the nations?

God's response about the Babylonians begins in verse 4. Before God pronounced their coming judgment, he once again described their character – drunken, proud, arrogant and greedy, and then five specific "woes" for five specific sins. Their day of reckoning would come. Tyrants, dictators, abusers and violators may prosper for a while and some may even escape judgment on earth but they will not escape God's judgment. Nations and their rulers will be judged as well as individuals, because power and position carries responsibility and accountability.

The five specific sins that the Babylonians would be judged

for were getting wealthy by plunder, extortion and wanton expansionism (verse 6), smug complacency in their impregnable city (verse 9), merciless violence and human exploitation (verse 12), drunken revelry and debauchery (verse 15), and useless idolatry (verse 19). It does not require any great imagination to see that these specific sins have a very definite counterpart in today's society.

But in the midst of these pronouncements of coming judgment, God gave the prophet three solid foundations for his faith to stand on at the time of national and international instability:

God's grace (verse 4) – *"the righteous person will live by his faith."*

When all around is being shaken and men's hearts are failing them for fear, the believer has an unshakeable foundation of the things that cannot be shaken.

God's glory (verse 14) – *"For the earth will be filled with the knowledge of the glory of the Lord as the waters cover the sea."*

God's people have the assurance that sin will not finally triumph in the world – the glory of God will eventually fill the earth.

God's government (verse 20) – *"But the Lord is in his holy temple; let all the earth be silent before him."*

God has not abdicated. The throne is still occupied and the purposes of God will finally triumph.

What a blessing Habakkuk received by waiting on the Lord. He got a powerful revelation of the certainty of future justice. It would take time but he could wait for the day with confidence, knowing that God would finally call the Babylonians to account. He was also reassured by promises about God's future glory and government which would allow him to live in faith while he waited.

I am sure he would be painfully aware of his misjudging of God. How wrong he had been to think that God wasn't listening or interested enough to do anything! God was at work, though not in a way Habakkuk would have expected. He may not have got all the explanations he wanted, but he got a revelation that was more than sufficient for him to live by.

An explanation may satisfy the need of a moment, but a revelation will provide a foundation for the rest of life.

11

From a Dirge to a Dance

- part four

———⚬———

Chapter 1 of Habakkuk finished with a question about the Babylonians and chapter 2 finished with a statement about God's omnipotence.

Habakkuk was being toughened up for the difficult days ahead when the Babylonians would invade and take the nation of Israel off into seventy years of captivity. His level of faith at the outset was good, but not sufficient for what lay ahead. As God took him on a journey of change in chapters 1 and 2, his faith began to steadily rise. But in chapter 3 it scales new heights and climaxes in one of the greatest statements of faith in the Bible.

The opening verse of the book states that Habakkuk received an oracle (a burden) from the Lord. We want God to share our burdens, but God also looks for people who will share his (see Colossians 1:24). In this journal, Habakkuk records his progression in receiving God's burden for the distressing events that would come on the people of God. In chapter 1, Habakkuk wrestled with a new concept of the ways of God that were beyond his current experience. In chapter 2, he climbed onto a lonely watchtower to patiently wait on God for help to understand what he was doing. Habakkuk was not disappointed and began to move into new dimensions of faith as the word of God was revealed to him. God chose not to change the circumstances of the prophet but the prophet's attitude to his circumstances was dramatically changed.

Chapter 3 is a musical chapter – the final verse sees the prophet calling for choir and orchestra to join him in extravagant praise. *"On shigionoth"* (chapter 3:1) means that the style of the music was to be "wild, enthusiastic and triumphal." What started out as a dirge of gloom and despair, changed dramatically to a wild, enthusiastic and triumphant song and dance.

Before the prophet launched into praise he started with prayer, no doubt inspired by what he had heard in chapter 2 – *"Lord, I have heard of your fame; I stand in awe of your deeds, O Lord. Repeat them in our day, in our time make them known; in wrath remember mercy."*

The prophet was aware of what God had done in the past, but he was not satisfied with his knowledge of history. He wanted to see God moving in his generation, and prayed for mercy even when they deserved wrath. His understanding of what God had done in the past inspired him to believe for what God would do in the present and the future.

The prayer is a big one, not taken up with pleas for preservation or provision but rooted in a vision of God's awesomeness. The prophet was trembling, and longing to see a renewal of God's power at this intersection of history.

After his revelation, Habakkuk was not transported to heaven in a chariot of fire; instead, he and the nation had to go through the awful trauma of an invasion, a siege and deportation. Yet he faced up to this with a new confidence in an all-powerful God who would still be at work in the situation. God does not always deliver us from difficult situations; sometimes he gives us grace to go through them with victory and confidence.

Chapter 3:3-15 are a remarkable replay of God's glory and power seen in Israel's history: the Exodus, the giving of the Law at Sinai, the crossing of the Red Sea, glory in the wilderness, times when God delivered his people by thunder, lightning, hailstones and floods and also when the sun stood still in the heavens for Joshua. As Habakkuk recalled these events, it seems that God was allowing him to see history through new eyes.

The effect of all this on the prophet was remarkable – heart pounding, lips quivering and legs trembling (chapter 3:16), he was physically shaken by the glory of God.

This chapter does not deserve to be rushed. "Selah," which means, "Stop and think about that," appears three times in the chapter. There are things that you need to stop and think about and if you do, the pause will deepen your understanding.

The last part of the chapter (verses 17-19) record one of the greatest statements of faith in the Bible. What a contrast from the despondency of the opening! The amazing thing is that for Habakkuk the circumstances had not changed – the invasion and deportation would still happen – but his whole attitude was different.

He was no longer focussed on negatives; his focus was now on the God who was infinitely bigger than the circumstances. In the midst of total economic collapse, there is a declaration of total confidence in God:

"I will rejoice in the Lord, I will be joyful in God my Saviour. The Sovereign Lord is my strength; he makes my feet like the feet of a deer, he enables me to tread on the heights." (Habakkuk 3:18-19)

As I have said before, we don't have a choice in what happens to us but we do have a choice in what we do with what happens to us. Habakkuk was faced with life-affecting challenges, but he made a choice to wait on God with patience. This led to revelation, followed by breakthrough prayer, and then extravagant confidence and praise.

12

A View From the Table

—⚏—

The Lord's Supper is sometimes called the Breaking of Bread, the Lord's Table or Holy Communion. Basically it is service of remembrance using the simplest of symbols – bread and wine or juice.

My father was an elder in South Dalziel Parish in Motherwell, Scotland, where communion was served four times a year. The bread and wine was distributed by the minister, from gleaming silverware on a dazzling white table cover, to forty-five elders wearing morning suits in white gloves, who then very solemnly served the people. The church was always full for the quarterly communion service.

In contrast to this very formal event, I have broken bread in some very basic conditions using whatever ingredients were to hand, and in whatever receptacles were available. The value of the moment is not increased or diminished by the surroundings or the ingredients.

Jesus knew how prone we all are to forget. On the night of his betrayal, he took time to institute a very simple but powerful service to aid our memories. He chose not to use complicated symbolism; rather he took the ingredients that were to hand, bread and wine and endowed them with new meaning. The broken bread spoke of his body to be broken, and the poured out wine spoke of his blood which was to be shed.

Regardless of how frequently or infrequently you take part in this simple service of remembrance, can I suggest four "views" from the table that might help make the time more meaningful?

1. Look back
At the table we look back to a death that happened more than 2000 years ago and so often our main focus is on the pain, the cruelty, the injustice and the betrayal. However, Jesus told us our main focus should be on him – *"Remember me."*

The night has been described as "the hour of darkness": treachery was in the air, and the disciples were at each other's throats, arguing about which of them was the greatest. Yet despite the atmosphere, Jesus gave thanks to God out of a spirit that was full of joy – *"for the joy that was set before him he endured the cross, scorning its shame."* Hebrews 12:2 goes on to tell us to be "fixing our eyes on Jesus." We look back to the cross with gratitude.

2. Look forward
Paul reminded the Corinthians that they would only take part in this remembrance service *"until he comes"* (1 Corinthians 11:6). There will come a time when a breaking of bread service will be the last one on earth, and then the Lord's Supper will be exchanged for the Marriage Supper. The service of remembrance is a foretaste of the time when the whole church, from every age, will be gathered together in his presence.

3. Look in

"A man ought to examine himself before he eats of the bread and drinks of the cup" (1 Corinthians 11:28). Though we should not be obsessed with introspection, regular "stock taking" is good for us. We should do this honestly and thoroughly, in the light of the cross and the promise that *"if we confess our sins he is faithful and just and will forgive us our sins and purify us from all righteousness"* (1 John 1:9).

4. Look around

We don't remember in isolation. From his broken body has come a new body that we are part of, the church of Jesus Christ, which includes all the believers of the fellowship we belong to and further afield.

Paul rebuked the Corinthians for their lack of consideration of fellow believers when they met together to break bread and remember the Lord (1 Corinthians 11:17–34). They were eating the bread and drinking the wine in an unworthy manner. Then he spoke of them not recognising the body of the Lord and the weakness and sickness that some had experienced, again in the context of relationships.

As we come to the table, it is good to examine our hearts about our relationship with the Lord, but also about our relationship with fellow believers.

The four "views" from the table are looking back to the Saviour's death on the cross, looking forward to his coming and the marriage supper of the Lamb, looking in to ensure that our walk with God is pleasing to him, and looking around to ensure that our relationship with the other members of his body is also good.

The table of remembrance is a good place to sharpen up our vision. Our eyes can lose concentrated focus but keeping sight of all four views can help us stay on track.

There may be moments at the table when the Holy Spirit may want you to focus particularly on one of the four views. Perhaps if life has become too controlled or dominated by your immediate affairs, then maybe the Spirit will remind you that there is much more to life than "now" – that there is a glorious future awaiting his people which will commence with the marriage supper.

13
Breakthrough, Not Breakdown

- part one

—ᴍ—

If you were allowed to ask one question to God which you knew he would answer, what would it be? Perhaps in the majority of responses the question would begin with, "Why?" There are so many unanswered questions and inexplicable life issues. Bad things happen to good people and also good things happen to bad people. Life can deal some hard blows to some people who do not deserve it.

Hebrews 11 gives a long list of people who received some amazing miracles from God but in verse 35 we are introduced to some who though commended for their faith and no doubt loved by God, did not receive what was promised and certainly caught a rough deal from life. To me one of the most attractive promises of the Bible is *"then I shall know fully even as I am fully known"* (1 Corinthians 13:12).

In this lesson we are introduced to one of the good kings of Israel who nevertheless suddenly faced a nation-threatening situation.

The story is found in 2 Chronicles 20 and the king was Jehoshaphat.

Chapter 20 opens with the words, "After this" which prompts the question, "after what?" So before we can go forward, we need to go back. The preceding three chapters give a quick overview of his life, and a clue to the reason for his success;

"The Lord was with Jehoshaphat because in his early days he walked in the ways that his father David had followed ... his heart was devoted to the ways of the Lord." (2 Chronicles 17:3, 6)

Jehoshaphat sent out teachers to instruct the nation in the ways of God, and the fear of God fell on surrounding nations.

In chapter 18, Jehoshaphat made a bad marriage alliance with Ahab, one of the most wicked kings of Israel. This was a bad move with bad consequences, but yes, sometimes good people make mistakes. However, in chapter 19 after a severe rebuke from a prophet, he repents and once more sends out godly teachers to the nation, even going out himself to teach the people the ways of God.

With this background we come to chapter 20:1-2 – *"After this, the Moabites and the Ammonites with some of the Meunites came to wage war against Jehoshaphat ... a vast army."*

Jehoshaphat could have thought, "This is a punishment for my mistake," or he could have complained, "Why is this happening to me?"

Often we ask similar questions, but God does not punish repentant people and the question, "Why?" while understandable, is not the best one. We would gain more by asking, "What?" – "What lesson is in this situation for me?" or "What opportunity to honour God could come out of this?"

However, this situation does raise the age-old question, "Why, when you have done your best to honour God, does something like this happen?"

This was a major crisis, 10+ on the Richter scale. But it wasn't just that the nation was being invaded, it was who was doing the invading. The Moabites were distant relatives on Esau's side of the family. Israel had shown them mercy on a previous occasion (Deuteronomy 2:2-6) so this was not a very nice way to repay the favour.

It is a sad fact that too many believers have been badly hurt by other members of God's family. King David knew about this pain –

"If an enemy were insulting me, I could endure it; if a foe were rising against me, I could hide. But it is you, a man like myself, my companion, my close friend, with whom I enjoyed sweet fellowship as we walked with the throng at the house of God." (Psalm 55:12-14)

It shouldn't happen, but it does.

Jehoshaphat's response

Maybe you have read the story of the police cadet who, during his training was asked for his response to a very complicated theoretical incident. His reply was, "Take off uniform and merge with crowd"!

How will Jehoshaphat respond – will it be flight or fight? Maybe he was tempted to look at an early retirement plan or an extended holiday away from Royal office. It's quite obvious from chapter 20 that he was very alarmed at the possibility of facing national annihilation.

So much about us is revealed by our responses. Too many get resentful and jealous of others who seem to be having a far easier time. Others get bitter and angry at God and walk off in a moody sulk, thereby missing the potential breakthrough that hides in every problem.

Habakkuk cried out to God at the beginning of his book, *"How long must I call for help, and you do not listen?"* but chapter 2 shows his response to an apparently absent God when he was sorely needed. Habakkuk climbed up onto a watchtower and settled down to get an answer from God about what was going on, and he ended up getting a far greater revelation of God.

God prefers to give revelation rather than explanation. There will be all of eternity for explanations but right now we are more in need of revelation. Although Habakkuk's problem did not go away, by the end of his book his appreciation of God's bigness cut the problem down to size.

We find a similar response in Jehoshaphat: *"Alarmed, Jehoshaphat resolved to enquire of the Lord, and proclaimed a fast."* This may have seemed a very strange way of fighting an invading army, but in the following chapter we will understand more about Jehoshaphat's breakthrough.

14

Breakthrough, Not Breakdown

- part two

—◊—

Character is revealed in a crisis: that's why God is more concerned about my character development than my comfort. Jehoshaphat revealed character when his nation was invaded by a huge foreign army and he *"resolved to enquire of the Lord"* (2 Chronicles 20:3). The whole nation joined him in fasting and seeking the help of God to deal with this crisis.

Before I became a pastor, I was in heavy pressure vessel engineering. At the end of the construction of a vessel it was essential that the product be put under major pressure to ensure it was fit for the task. Any leaks and it was back to the workshop.

I heard the story of a man who was watching a butterfly emerge from its chrysalis. As he watched the struggle, he decided to lend a hand and help it get out. Unfortunately thereafter the butterfly was unable to fly because the struggle to emerge was the way its wing muscles were strengthened to enable it to fly.

It has been said that, "Life is 20% what happens to you and 80% what you do with what happens to you." We are going to look at the choices Jehoshaphat made in this crisis through 2 Chronicles chapter 20.

Prayer

The king led the nation in passionate prayer, beginning by reminding himself and the people of the power of the God they were praying to. He also remembered God's promise, *"If we cry out to you in our distress you will hear us and save us."*

Jehoshaphat was also mindful of the nation's history, especially in relation to the invaders, the Moabites. He finished with a declaration of their complete helplessness: *"We have no power to face this vast army that is attacking us. We do not know what to do but our eyes are upon you."* What a prayer! What a model for our prayers – God's power, his promises, God at work in history and our complete helplessness without his intervention.

Prophecy

Imagine the scene – the whole nation, including children, standing silently before the Lord. Suddenly the Spirit of the Lord came on a man in the large congregation called Jahaziel. Although the writer gives his long family pedigree, we know nothing about him before and after the event.

The Spirit gave Jahaziel great boldness, and in front of the king and all the royal officials as well as the whole nation, he loudly spoke out a very strong word from God.

The prophecy gave them all God's directive word for the way ahead – *"Do not be afraid or discouraged because of this vast army. For the battle is not yours but God's"* (2 Chronicles 20:15).
God then gave them specific instructions about what they had to do the next day.

The effect of the prophecy was immediate – the king and the whole nation fell on their knees before God in worship. His word galvanised them all into obedient action and changed the national mood from fear to faith, from crisis to confidence. There is nothing in this world like a word from God; it is more powerful than any vast army or life-threatening situation. It is well worth waiting and seeking to receive it.

Praise

It started in a section of the congregation, when the Levites stood up and with very loud voices began to praise God. The praise continued into the next day as the people marched out to face their enemies. The men out in front began to sing, *"Give thanks to the Lord, for his love endures for ever,"* and the refrain was picked up by all those following.

What a strange sight – a whole nation going out to face their enemies and led, not by the strongest men, but by the loudest singers of praise to God. This praise started before the battle and before the victory, in fact it assisted in the victory – *"As they began to sing and praise, the Lord set ambushes against [the invaders]."*

When Jehoshaphat and the people got to the battleground, what a sight met them! Not a man of the invading army was left standing: they had all turned on each other and destroyed each other. All the people had to do was carry off the plunder and then return home with a song of thanksgiving – the song of praise before the battle leads to the song of thanksgiving after the battle.

I hope by now you cannot wait to get your Bible out and read this amazing story for yourself!

One of the big life lessons in this story is that living to please God will not always mean you are exempt from the attacks of the enemy. We may not be protected from attacks, but we certainly can be protected in them. It is worth remembering that the attack will sometimes come through unexpected people. You have a choice as to how you will respond, and that response will affect the outcome.

From Jehoshaphat we learn the power of passionate prayer, the joy of a word from God and the effect that praise can have. We may not want to praise God for the situation, but we certainly can praise him in the situation, and in this story praise played a big part in the victory.

15

Chameleons, Caterpillars and Butterflies

- part one

—m—

We all have our favourite preachers, and when I was a young minister, David Pawson was my ideal. I loved his clear thinking and amazing illustrations. He came to Cardiff to preach at an Easter Convention and I still remember his opening illustration for his sermon on Romans 12:1-2 – "Don't be a chameleon, be a caterpillar."

If you are familiar with the verses you will remember that Paul said, *"Do not conform to the pattern of this world, but be transformed."* A chameleon conforms itself to its surrounding colour but a butterfly is the result of metamorphosis – it is transformed from an earth-bound caterpillar to a beautiful butterfly capable of flight. The point he was making was that we must not conform to the shape and tone of this world but to be transformed by the renewing of our minds.

I once used this illustration in a rural area of Africa where I said that if the chameleon sits on blue it will turn blue, and if it sits on brown it will turn brown, but if you put it on tartan it will burst – it can't handle tartan! The illustration was going well till I got to the word tartan, and then the interpreters launched into a big discussion about how to explain tartan. It took several minutes and the story was ruined!

Romans 12, especially the first two verses, will be our focus for the next three chapters so, read it for yourself when you get the chance.

Paul's letter to the Romans

Paul had a clear mission strategy for taking the gospel to the known world. He concentrated on key cities and after preaching the gospel he would gather the converts together, teach them the basics of the Christian life, appoint elders over them and commission them all to evangelise the city, district and region they lived in. He would then move on and repeat the procedure in another key city.

In the midst of this highly effective strategy, Paul nursed a burning ambition to go to Rome and preach the gospel right in the heart of the Roman Empire, perhaps even to Caesar himself (See Acts 19:21). To prepare for his desired visit to Rome he wrote his letter to the Roman Christians by way of an introduction of himself and the gospel he preached. Paul did eventually reach Rome, though not the way he expected; he arrived as a prisoner facing trial before Caesar (see Acts 28:14).

Rather than dealing with church problems, this book is pure theology. In it Paul follows his usual pattern of writing – by first giving a specific teaching followed by the practical application of the teaching. Paul was very strong on the indivisible relationship of belief and behaviour. You cannot have belief in isolation; it must be accompanied by changed behaviour and just as what we really believe is seen by how we behave, so how we behave is conditioned by what we believe – "What God has joined together, let not man separate."

The theme of the teaching section, the first 11 chapters, is summed up in chapter 12:1 – *"God's mercy."* In the first 11 chapters Paul's great academic mind had wrestled with complex theological problems as he expounded the theme of the mercy of God expressed in salvation for Jews and Gentiles, but finally he goes as far as he can to fathom it out.

Theology becomes doxology (an expression of glory to God)

When Paul comes to the end of his ability to explain, all that is left is to stand back in awe and amazement at God's unsearchable mercy in salvation. Chapter 11:32-36 is Paul's outpouring of praise to God. Paul has used his mind to try and explain God's mercy but now his soul is pouring out worship to God. After praising God, Paul then outlines how an understanding of the mercy of God should affect a person's life.

Mercy must produce a response in us

"Therefore, I urge you, brothers and sisters, in view of God's mercy..."

When I was a student I was told that when you see a "therefore," you should ask the question "What's it there for?" The "therefore" in verse 1 connects all that follows with all that has gone before – in the light of all we have read about God's incredible salvation these then are the measurable changes that should begin to be obvious in daily life and behaviour.

As we begin to understand even in a limited way God' unfathomable mercy to us, we can no longer go on living an old way of life. It must produce a change in us. If there is no change then the unavoidable conclusion is that there has been no understanding or experience of God's mercy.

One of the important areas of measurable response will be in our worship. Shortly we will see three significant responses that Paul describes as *"true and proper worship."* An alternative reading calls it a *"reasonable act of worship."* Worship, for so many, has been devalued to merely singing. It does include music but it is far more than that.

A helpful guide for understanding a Bible subject is "the law of first mention" – look for the first mention of the subject and it will help give a clearer insight into its unpolluted meaning.

To find the first mention of "worship" in the Bible, we have to go right back to Genesis chapter 22 where Abraham is challenged by God to sacrifice his first-born son. Rising early, Abraham, Isaac and the servants travel to the place of sacrifice. When they arrive Abraham asks the servants to wait behind as he and Isaac go further: *"We will worship and then we will come back to you."*

Abraham's worship was prompt and total obedience to God, even to the offering of his most precious possession – *"Isaac, his son, his only son, whom he loved."* What a totally fresh and uncomplicated understanding of worship this gives us. In the next chapter we will see three distinctive characteristics of *"true and proper worship".*

16

Chameleons, Caterpillars and Butterflies

- part two

—⫘—

When Moses stood before Pharaoh, he stated God's demand: *"Let my people go so that they may worship me"* (Exodus 7:16). God wanted to transform his people from slave workers to worshippers. Jesus said that the Father is seeking worshippers (John 4:23-24).

God first and foremost is seeking worshippers, not workers. Those who truly worship God will also work for him, but it starts with worship. In the last chapter we looked at the original use of the word "worship," and saw that for Abraham it meant prompt and total obedience of God, even when the cost was very painful.

In Romans 12:1-2 Paul is talking about what defines worship and gives us three evidences of a life marked by it – physical, social and spiritual evidences that are measurable and visible.

1.Make a present of your body to God (physical)

The Greeks of Paul's day saw the body as a necessary evil and not something of any value. In their eyes, what you did with your body did not matter. Paul however, made it very clear that what we do with our body does matter – it is a temple for the Holy Spirit and as such has to be treated as part of our worship.

This "once and for all" gift of our body to God is to be a living sacrifice of the every-day activities of our life. This presenting of our bodies has to be done willingly, as an act of love. It will include all the mundane and physical actions of every day – what we look at, where we go, what we touch, the use of our tongues, how we use our time and energy, our life at work, at home and in our neighbourhood.

This challenges the false "sacred versus secular" divide which breaks life up into different compartments, with some more important than others. What we do with our bodies on a Saturday night is as significant as what we do with them on a Sunday morning. To God the workplace is as sacred as the church meeting place.

2. Refuse to be conformed to this world's ways (social)

This world has loose-leaf ethics dictated and controlled by personal advantage and changing situations, but for the Christian, ethics, standards, values and behaviour are not shaped by this world. J B Philip summed it up in his translation of verse 2, *"Don't let this world press you into its mould."*

Sadly the demarcation line between God's people and the world can sometimes be very narrow – deception, lies, dishonesty and cheating have now become a normal part of life and we now even have television programmes based on how skilled people are at lying. The outward standards and culture of this world are always changing, but we worship God by choosing not to be conformed to this world's standards.

"Do not be conformed..." is not debatable; it is a command from the Holy Spirit. God wants us to be attractively different to the people of this world; living lives that make people ask questions.

Paul's teaching to slaves was that they should live such good lives that they would, *"make the teaching about God our Saviour attractive"* (Titus 2:10).

There are three ways that Christ is fully presented to the world:

1. By proclamation – the use of words: what people hear.
2. By demonstration – signs, wonders, miracles: what people feel.
3. By illustration – the power of transformed lives: what people see.

Daring to be attractively different to the people of this world is one of our ways of worshipping God.

3. Be transformed by the renewing of your mind (spiritual)

This is worshipping God with a renewed way of thinking. Conformed has to do with the outward but transformed has do with what is inside. The word that is used here is a familiar one, "metamorphose," which means to change from one state to another.

This word reminds us of one of the most beautiful and amazing miracles of nature, the transformation of a caterpillar into a butterfly. The miracle has three stages – caterpillar, chrysalis and butterfly and each stage has something to teach us:

• *The caterpillar stage*
The caterpillar is very much an earth-bound creature. It is slow moving, not too pretty to look and a ravenous eating machine that can do a lot of damage. But inside it has the potential for something better, to be more than just a consumer.

• *The chrysalis stage*
To achieve its destiny, the caterpillar must go through a time of severe restriction. For some species this period will only last a few months, while for other species of butterfly it can last much longer, but in this time of darkness a miracle of transformation is taking place.

Exodus 20:21 is a fascinating verse, *"The people remained at a distance, while Moses approached the thick darkness where God was."* How strange to find God in the thick darkness! But on the other side of the darkness, Moses met God and when he emerged from the experience his face was shining. There are some frightening dark and limiting experiences that we would naturally shrink from, but they can be part of a transformation time that leads to a greater destiny.

There are many biblical examples of people who had to go through a chrysalis experience before they emerged transformed. Joseph was a slave in an Egyptian prison and then emerged as Prime Minister. John the Baptist spent almost three decades in a wilderness before he emerged as the forerunner of Christ.

Paul took time out in Arabia and obscurity before he emerged as a providentially prepared apostle for the Gentiles. The three Hebrew young men chose to burn rather than bow, but in the fire they met and walked with the fourth man. God's promise in Isaiah 45:3 is reassuring – *"I will give you the treasures of darkness, riches stored in secret places."*

In the next chapter we will observe the third stage – the butterfly emerging – and also look at what is meant by the "renewing of our minds."

17

Chameleons, Caterpillars and Butterflies

- part three

—ɯ—

There is no short cut between the caterpillar stage and the butterfly stage; for a caterpillar to become a butterfly it has to go through the chrysalis stage. This will mean restriction, limitation and darkness which is necessary for there to be a change to a completely new form of life.

Sometimes the process of sanctification and preparation for special service can seem a lot like the chrysalis experience, but the final outcome makes it worthwhile.

• *The butterfly stage*

After the struggle of the chrysalis stage, what had been an earth-bound caterpillar now emerges as a beautiful butterfly capable of flight.

Paul knew a lot about suffering and restrictions but said, *"our light and momentary troubles are achieving for us an eternal glory that far outweighs them all"* (2 Corinthians 4:16-17).

Job said after his chrysalis experience, *"my ears had heard of you but now my eyes have seen you"* (Job 42:5). Jacob wrestled with God for a whole night but the "grasper" came out of it as a new man: "Israel."

The mind is the key to transformation

"Be transformed by the renewing of your mind." (Romans 12:2)

The god of this world wants to control our minds but God wants to renew them. The mind is crucial to so much – *"As a man thinks in his heart so is he."* Out of thoughts come our assessments, values, opinions and attitudes, which control our actions and lifestyle. An attitude affects how we behave, so how we think is crucial. Therefore when our thinking is transformed, our whole way of living will be affected.

The Holy Spirit works with the word so that our minds can be transformed into the attitude of Christ. This change of thinking will be seen in how we think about God, ourselves, other believers and people in the world, even those who persecute us.

Romans 12:3–21 gives some detail on the practical outworking of this new way of thinking. This is transformation from the inside, working its way out into everyday life. The transformation will be so impressive (just like the caterpillar changing to a butterfly) that people will not fail to see the evidence of a changed life.

Our thinking about God will be different, no longer dominated by fear, dread or apathy. Now we look up to the face of a heavenly Father who has displayed such mercy to us and we worship him with transformed lives.

Our thinking about ourselves will also be affected. We live in a "Because you are worth it," "me-centred" generation, but because of grace we are now to think soberly, with an honest faith-controlled assessment of ourselves, unlike the alcohol-fuelled delusions of a drunk man. We now have an attitude of service – each of us is a gift to the body of Christ with a part to play and a ministry to contribute.

We are gifted, not to enhance our standing or reputation, but to edify the body of Christ. Romans 12:4-8 gives a list of some of those gifts we can bless others with, but there are more. Our attitudes are now to be selfless – we no longer just belong to ourselves but *"each member belongs to all the others"* (Romans 12:5). But the revolution in thinking is not over.

Our thinking about people in the world also will be changed, especially towards persecutors – *"Bless those who persecute you ... Do not repay anyone evil for evil ... Do not take revenge ... If your enemy is hungry, feed him"* (Romans 12:14, 17, 19, 20) – what a totally transformed way of thinking and behaving!

So the "good, pleasing and perfect will of God" (Romans 12:2) has to be tested and approved, not in a forum for academics but rather on the test bed of daily life. The will of God which is good, pleasing and perfect can be seen in a revolutionised attitude towards God – we will gladly present our bodies to him as living sacrifices which we will look on as reasonable worship.

The will of God will also be tested and proved by our refusal to be conformed like chameleons to this world's way of thinking or living. It will also pass the test as being good, pleasing and perfect when we are delivered from selfish thinking and living.

But as far as the world is concerned, the most arresting demonstration will be seen in a totally illogical attitude of love towards the people of this world, especially towards those who persecute us. The most measurable test that a person has received and understood the mercy of God is that they themselves become merciful, especially towards those who do not deserve it.

These then are the evidences of reasonable and spiritual worship that Paul urges the believers at Rome to display in their transformed lives. Not like chameleons taking their colour and standards from those around them, but like beautiful butterflies with new natures and transformed lives for the glory of God.

18

Follow Me

- part one

—◊◊◊—

When Jesus said "Follow me," it was not an invitation to join a new religion or a particular brand of denomination or church. He was inviting people to enter into a life-long journey of developing intimacy with him.

Becoming a Christian is very personal. This is one of the facts that make Christianity so unique among world religions – our God is not remote or distant. He wants a personal relationship with each of his followers which is alive and progressive.

Once, on a trip to Thailand, a missionary friend of mine took me to visit a temple which contained what can only be described as a supermarket for idols. People could select an idol of choice from a large selection of idols of various sizes, materials and appearance, then pay at the check-out, take it home and set it up for worship. This is galaxies removed from becoming a worshipper of God.

Peter discovered that responding to Christ's "Follow me" certainly was a life-transforming experience. His journey took him through a series of challenges that stretched him more than anything he had ever before experienced.

We are going to look at four episodes in Peter's journey of following Christ, but at the start of this study, think about your own journey of following Christ. Could it be described as stuck, side-tracked, or stale? Or is it stretching and satisfying?

We have made discipleship very complicated, with so many "hoops" for believers to jump through to feel they are making the grade. Maybe we have lost the straightforward simplicity of a daily walk with Christ.

Arthur Burns, a Jewish Senator, was once asked to close in prayer at a Whitehouse prayer meeting, this was his prayer: "Lord, I pray that you bring Jews to know Jesus Christ. I pray that you would bring Muslims to know Jesus Christ. Finally, Lord, I pray that you would bring Christians to know Jesus Christ." Very perceptive!

(1) Following Christ – the beginning

Peter was a business man in partnership with his own boat; life for him and his family would be better than for most others but two words from Jesus changed his life for ever. The incident in Luke 5 was not his first encounter with Jesus – the Lord had previously been to his home and healed his mother-in-law.

In Luke 5 Jesus was teaching multitudes of people by the Sea of Galilee. Peter and the other fishermen were mending their nets while he was preaching. Peter was listening but still working – was he so busy? Or maybe he didn't want it to appear that he was too interested.

Jesus narrowed that gap when he asked to use his boat to preach from. Then they launched out into deep water, where he got Peter away from the crowd for a one-to-one encounter that culminated in the life-changing words – *"Follow me...and I will make you fishers of men"* (Mark 1:17).

If Peter would do the following, Jesus would do the making. It's still the same today; if we will follow he will make us into something we are not, but if we won't follow he can't make anything of us. The closer we follow, the more he can make of us.

"Follow me" was not a proposal for discussion or a suggestion for debate. It was (and still is) a command with only one of two possible answers – "Yes, I will follow," or "No, I will not." There was no negotiation on terms and conditions or examination of the small print to see what the package included.

When a person declares Jesus Christ to be their Lord, he becomes just that, their Lord – the one who has total authority over their life. To say yes is to acknowledge Christ as the supreme authority over every part of life. When Peter spoke that word, "Lord," (Luke 5:8) it was a life-transforming moment. I think he had a moment of fear as he faced this defining choice, because Jesus told him not to be afraid and then said, *"From now on you will catch men."*

Peter and James and John pulled their boat up on the shore and left everything to follow Christ. Little did they comprehend the far-reaching and world-affecting consequences of that defining moment. It was the start of the most exciting, demanding, painful, and meaningful journey of their lives. It would lead to the greatest suffering and the greatest glory, the greatest cost and the greatest reward. This would affect Peter's personal life, his business life, his family life and his spiritual life.

Many people today are finding that success is not enough; they want to be significant. Steve Covey in his book, *The Seven Habits of Highly Effective People*, states four purposes of a life – "To live, to learn, to love and to leave a legacy," – to feel that when you die you have left something worthwhile behind.

This must have been an exciting moment for Peter, who was burning his boats behind him to embark on a journey with Christ but it wasn't something that had gripped Peter it was someone. He was leaving the safe, the predictable and the secure for the start of his greatest life venture.

(2) Following Christ – the need for a course correction

By Matthew 19, Peter was well into following Jesus. He had become one of his prominent disciples, but little did he realise that an attitude had developed within him that needed correcting. An unexpected event brought it to the surface.

A man presented himself to Jesus and asked the question, *"Teacher, what good thing must I do to get eternal life?"* This man had the three things that are highly prized by most people – he was young, he was rich and he had authority. He was a ruler but he was unsatisfied with his life, and recognised that there was something missing.

The next chapter will show what Jesus said to this young man, but also how he dealt with Peter's hidden bad attitude.

19
Follow Me

- part two

—〰—

There are peculiar dangers for those who have been on the discipleship road for a while. Peter was unaware of a potentially dangerous attitude that had developed in him; the visit of the rich young man brought it to the surface.

Jesus answered the young man's question, *"What good thing must I do to inherit eternal life."* The young man was sincere, but his answer showed that he was unwilling to surrender his wealth to follow Jesus, so he went away unchanged and very sad.

As the young man walked away, Jesus took the opportunity to say some important things to his disciples about the power and the danger of wealth. At this point, Peter asked, *"We have left everything to follow you! What then will there be for us?"* (Matthew 19:27). Can you detect the subtle attitude problem? Peter may have been comparing his willingness with the rich young man's unwillingness but in any case, a bargaining spirit had crept in:

"What reward will we get for sacrifice?"

Jesus first answered his question and then answered the attitude behind the question. In Matthew 19:28-29 Jesus makes it clear that the personal sacrifices made for the sake of the Kingdom of God will be far outweighed by the glory that lies ahead.

Then Jesus answered Peter's attitude with an industrial relations story (Matthew 20:1-16). A landowner needed casual labour to work his vineyard, so at six in the morning he went to the local labour exchange and made a contract with some men for a day's wage for a day's work. Later at 9am, 12 noon, and 5pm, he found more men willing to work for what was left of the day, but no contract was agreed regarding the rate of pay.

The problem started at the end of the day when the men were paid, beginning with those who had worked the least hours. They were given a full day's wage for less than a full day's work and were amazed at the landowner's generosity.

Then it came to the men who had borne the heat of the day and given the most labour. They assumed that they would receive a bonus, but no, they got what had been agreed, a day's wage for a day's work. Understandably, that's when the protests of unfairness began. The landowner made it clear that he was at liberty to be as generous as he liked regards payment, but those who had worked for a contract got their legal rights.

The point Jesus was making to Peter and the other disciples was that working in the Kingdom is not governed by legal rights – it is a kingdom of grace. There are no shop stewards negotiating terms and conditions or levels of pay based on seniority. It is the rewards of grace, not the payment of wages for time and sacrifice given.

God is our Father, not our employer, and when we stand in glory and receive the promised rewards we will be so overwhelmed by his grace, not our labour, that the rewards will be thrown at his feet in adoration.

So, the answer to Peter's question, *"What then will there be for us?"* is far more than we deserve. What we have given up will be eclipsed in the realisation of what he gave up.

A big lesson in this story is the importance of us not taking ourselves too seriously or being overly impressed by our own talents, seniority or sacrifices. At our best, we are "sinners saved by grace." We are called to have a great sense of his importance and a very realistic understanding of ours.

Those who have been in Kingdom work for a long time can be tempted to imagine that it brings special privileges. What it does bring is extra responsibility and an enlarged awareness of his amazing grace. Jesus summed it up when he told the disciples –

"So you also, when you have done everything you were told to do, should say, 'We are unworthy servants; we have only done our duty'." (Luke 17:10)

It's not too hard to begin the Christian life overwhelmed by grace, but to keep following with that same sense of amazement as the decades pass is a rare ability.

(3) Following Christ – even when the going gets tough – Mark 10:32-34

"They were on their way up to Jerusalem, with Jesus leading the way, and the disciples were astonished, while those who followed were afraid." (Mark 10:32)

Why were they astonished, and what made them afraid?

This was Jesus' last journey to Jerusalem before he died. Three times he warned his disciples of what lay ahead – betrayal, condemnation, mocking, flogging, abuse and ultimately death. This was not what they had anticipated would happen; they were looking for a powerful Kingdom with themselves as senior ministers in it.

Now they were seeing an aspect of Jesus they had never seen before and they did not like it. He was saying things they did not understand and he had a very determined look on his face, so it was no wonder they were astonished and afraid. But they were still following.

The challenge from this stage in Peter's journey is to keep following even when things are not going the way you want. Read on for more on this and then the last stage of Peter's following of Christ.

20

Follow Me

- part three

—⚏—

Peter and the other disciples were astonished and afraid (Mark 10:32) but they were still following Jesus. At this stage of Peter's journey with Jesus, we recognise the challenge to maintain commitment to Christ despite adverse circumstances.

There is a lot of misleading teaching today that denies the reality of the Christian life. Jesus never promised that following him would be the best life-enhancing decision a person would ever make. In fact, he told his followers that they could expect tribulation and could lose their possessions and even their lives, things that are a daily reality for many believers in the world today. This certainly does not tie in with the promises made by the "prophets of plenty" who often make very large personal incomes from their unbalanced teaching.

In John 6 Jesus preached a sermon on the bread of life. At the beginning he had a very large audience of listeners, but by the end he was left with his twelve disciples. What could he have said that offended so many who apparently were his followers?

At the beginning of the sermon the people responded positively – *"What must we do to do the works God requires?"* This was a good start, but as he moved on, there was another response – *"From now on, give us this bread."* As the teaching became more demanding, *"the Jews began to grumble."* Soon, they *"began to argue sharply among themselves,"* and finally, *"From that time many of his disciples turned back and no longer followed him."*

This sermon followed the feeding of the multitude and as a result of that miracle the crowds wanted to make Jesus king by force (John 6:15). They liked the idea of a king who could miraculously feed multitudes – after all if he could do that, what more could he do? Jesus had to make the cost of discipleship very clear. It wasn't going to be all free meals and a miraculous answer to their national aspirations.

In Matthew 24, Jesus warned of three things that would profoundly challenge every one of his followers: persecution, deception and wickedness. In fact, he declared that in the last days many, if not most, would be caught out by one or more of the three tests. We must all settle this matter in our hearts once and for all – "Am I committed and determined to follow him no matter what the circumstances are?"

(4) Following Christ – the start of a new beginning

By John 21, Peter had gone through a profound breaking experience. His confident assertion that nothing would ever stop him following Christ had been demolished by a few words from a servant girl. His resolve had crumbled and he denied his Lord three times.

For the disciples, the cross had shattered their carefully constructed expectations, but now Jesus was alive and something totally new seemed to be happening. Another fruitless fishing expedition culminated in Peter jumping into the water and swimming to the shore to meet Jesus, where he was met by the smell of fresh bread and fish cooking on hot coals.

It's hard to take in the fact that Jesus, after all the world-affecting events of his death and resurrection, took time to cook breakfast for a hurting disciple. But after breakfast it was time for a very personal one-to-one interview. With three painful questions, Jesus showed Peter what following him in the future was going to cost and made the same challenge of years before – *"Follow me."*

This time, though, Peter was making his decision with full knowledge of the implications. At this point he did what many of us tend to do when an interview gets too pointed – he tried to divert attention on to someone else, saying, *"Lord, what about him?"* But the Lord would not let him off the hook – *"What is that to you? You must follow me."*

There comes a point in each person's Christian walk that they must decide to follow Jesus in full knowledge of the cost, and regardless of the Lord's plans for others.

This was Peter's final break with his old way of life and self confidence. Instead he was choosing to follow Jesus in total dependence on the Lord's strength.

"Follow me"

Maybe you are still near the beginning and the adventure is still fresh. Or perhaps you are in need of a course correction, because some unhelpful attitudes need dealing with.

Some may need to commit to following, despite the fact that the going is tough. Others are facing a serious decision to commit to following when in full possession of the facts regarding the cost. But to follow him is still the greatest privilege in life.

21

A Prophet Who Loved Profit

- part one

—✶—

The following two phrases will introduce one of the most contradictory characters in the entire Bible. His story is very much out of the ordinary.

The narrative of this man begins in Numbers but he is also mentioned in Deuteronomy, Joshua, Nehemiah, Micah, 2 Peter, Jude and Revelation. He is never spoken of in a good way but is universally condemned for moral, ethical and spiritual failings.

The following two phrases reflect the themes of his story:

- Be glad when God says "no" in love
- Beware when God says "yes" in anger

No is as much an answer as yes, though it is seldom the one we want. Children are expert manipulators at getting the wanted "yes" from their parents, and have an armoury of weapons that they know how to use to great effect. However, parents who truly love their children know that sometimes enforcing a "no" is the best way of showing love for their children.

Jesus pleaded with his Father to save him from the horrors of the cross, but the Father's will prevailed, and we are the long-term beneficiaries of that divine "no."

Paul pleaded three times for God to remove his "thorn in the flesh," the messenger of Satan, but God's refusal opened up for Paul a reservoir of grace that was more than sufficient. In addition, Paul was protected from the dangers of his amazing revelations. God said "no" in love.

The prophet who loved profit

Numbers 22 introduces the person we are going to focus on – Balaam. He could best be described as a spiritual medium, a prophet for hire. He was willing to work with any local, national or international deity as long as the price was right.

Balaam's true loyalty was to Mammon, the god of greed and avarice. He was the forerunner of the spiritual charlatans and quacks who fleece many people today. Unfortunately some of them claiming to be Christians earn for themselves obscene sums of money in return for confusion and disappointment.

Balaam gets hired

The background to this saga was Israel's deliverance from slavery in Egypt, but because of unbelief they had spent 40 years wandering in the wilderness. During that time they had changed from a rabble of slaves into a vast organised worshipping community with a health and hygiene system that was way ahead of its day.

Because of a communication system involving trumpets, the vast community could be packed up and on the move in a very short space of time.

And right in the heart of their well organised camp stood the tabernacle with the symbol of the presence of God hovering over it – a cloud by day and a pillar of fire by night. When they were camped or on the move they were an awe-inspiring nation and our story opens with one nation's fear and dread of this vast horde of people who had camped on their doorstep.

The solution for Moab's king, Balak, was an alliance with Midian. The two new allies sent a message to the internationally acclaimed pagan prophet Balaam to come and put a curse on this invading nation. Those are the headlines, but Numbers 22 gives the full story.

Balaam's attempt to earn his fee for divination

It is important to remember that God was aware of all that was hidden in the heart of Balaam, not just the pious and apparently correct words that came out of his mouth. On the surface he appears to be very spiritual, but from an awareness of the whole story we know that he was a spiritual fraud, a pagan prophet who was really only interested in profit.

When the king's envoys arrived, Balaam took time to check out what God wanted and the will of God was made very clear: *"Do not go with them"* (Numbers 22:12). When other more dignified envoys arrived with the offer of an even bigger fee, he went back to God, no doubt hoping for a change of mind.

From Numbers 22:20 it appears that God did change his mind and Balaam is given permission to go with them, albeit with the warning that he would not be able to do what he pleased. Was this unexpected "yes" a test? Or was God so aware of Balaam's determination to go and get the fee for divination that we have an example of God saying "yes" in anger?

The talking donkey

As with the story of Jonah, many are aware of the dramatic headlines but ignorant of the message behind them. God was angered by Balaam's haste to get to Moab and an angel was dispatched to oppose him.

It's incredible that a donkey had more vision than this sought-after prophet.

The donkey saved his life by avoiding the angel with the drawn sword and three times Balaam beat it until bizarrely, the donkey was forced to speak. Interestingly, Balaam did not appear fazed by the fact that he was holding a conversation with his animal! Facing an angel with a drawn sword obviously put a healthy fear of God into Balaam, if only temporarily. He realised that he was not dealing with some minor local deity. His life was in danger and he took care as to how he proceeded.

Finally Balaam arrived at a very anxious and impatient King Balak of Moab who again dangled a fat fee for cursing Israel in front of him. As far as the king was concerned, it was time for Balaam to do something to earn his fee.

22

A Prophet Who Loved Profit

- part two

—ɯ—

As Balak demanded action from his temporary employee, the king was no doubt concerned to hear him declare that he would not be in control over what he said – Balaam now had a healthy fear of not offending the God of the Israelites. What a pity that this fear was not the beginning of wisdom to control his later actions.

Balak did all he thought was necessary for the casting of a curse and so altars were built and sacrifices made. Then it was the turn of Balaam to engage in his pagan incantations (see Numbers 24:1) which underline the mixed-up and contradictory confusion of this man's spirituality.

King Balak attempted to get Israel cursed at three different sites, no doubt hoping that each new place would be more conducive to Balaam's sorcery. Yet on each occasion, when Balaam opened his mouth, all that came out were words of praise and blessing on Israel. It is well worth a read of Numbers 23 and 24 to feel the impact of what was being said by Balaam.

Finally Balak exploded with frustration and anger (see Numbers 24:10-11), sacked Balaam and sent him away minus his fee. Balaam's parting shot was a final oracle foretelling the coming of the Messiah. You might be wondering how such a wonderful prophecy could come through the mouth of this rogue prophet!

Well, if God can speak through a dumb donkey, he can certainly use the mouth of Balaam. After all, the source of the words is God; Balaam was only a mouthpiece. John 11:49-51 tells us that the high priest Caiaphas made a remarkable prophecy about one man dying for the people. As an opponent of Christ he certainly wasn't a worthy mouthpiece.

Now that seemed to be the end of the matter – Israel was blessed, not cursed. Balaam went home unpaid, but from a careful reading of what follows, it certainly was not the end of the matter.

Beware when God says "yes" in anger

Balaam was engaged to curse the people of God, but God had forbidden him from doing this. If only he had moved on from that point, who knows how significant his ministry could have been. After all, this pagan prophet had a powerful encounter with God, personally witnessed the amazing sign of a talking donkey and saw a mighty angel with a drawn sword sent to oppose him.

The word of God was so close to him. It was even in his mouth and yet his final end was death along with the enemies of God's people. God gave him permission to go to Moab while he was prevented from getting the handsome reward the King had promised.

When God says "no" but we push for a "yes," we are in danger of him abandoning us to the consequences of our own determination. After all, God is not a tyrant; he respects the free will he has given us. The best and safest prayer we can consistently pray is for his will to be done on earth (and in our lives) in the same way that it is done in heaven.

We need to be prepared for the unwanted "no" from God.

The mature believer will receive it as the right answer from an all-wise and all-loving heavenly Father who wants only the long-term best for his children.

When Hezekiah was told he was going to die he went into a big sulk with God for more time. Finally God relented and extended his life by 15 years, but they were certainly not his finest era. The record of his reign would have been better if he had accepted God's original will.

Balaam finally gets his reward from King Balak

Numbers 25 is a very sad chapter in the account of Israel's journey to the Promised Land. It tells of a subtle change of tactics by Balak – instead of trying to defeat Israel militarily or curse them, he made friends with them. He invited them to come and have meals with his people and got his young girls to dress alluringly to tempt the Israeli boys. In a frighteningly short space of time, Israel's holiness was compromised.

The Israelite young men were seduced by Moabite young women who invited them to pagan sacrifices, and they ended up in sexually immoral behaviour. One of the vital ingredients for Israel's safety was her separation from the gross immorality and spiritual perversion of the inhabitants of the land, and right on the eve of crossing over to the Promised Land, this was compromised.

Numbers 25 records the judgment of God on the nation for their sin and 24,000 people died as a consequence. But when we go over to Numbers 31, we see the judgment of God on the nation that seduced Israel and learn a startling fact – the person behind Midian and Moab's change of tactics is none other than Balaam.

Numbers 31:8 tells us that Balaam was among the recorded dead after God's punishment on Midian; the wages of sin is death and that's exactly what he got. We also learn from Numbers 31:16 that it was on his advice that Moab and Midian changed tactics. By seducing Israel they could have destroyed the people of God on the eve of crossing into Canaan:

"They were the ones who followed Balaam's advice and were the means of turning the Israelites away from the Lord in what happened at Peor, so that a plague struck the Lord's people."

The advice of this corrupt prophet almost worked, severely weakening God's people, but the wrath of God finally fell on him and the nation who took his advice. Balaam had inside information and knew how advantageous his advice could be to Moab and how potentially disastrous it could be to the people of God. He seems to have been determined to get the reward from Balak by one way or another.

23

A Prophet Who Loved Profit

- part three

—⚍—

Balaam is referred to in five different books in the Old Testament and three in the New Testament, where very stark and clear messages are culled from his life. He is held up as a serious warning to believers. His previous life had been sorcery, incantations and involvement with false gods and idols, but for a short time he had encountered the living and true God. However, the lure of money proved too strong for him as his corrupt nature overcame his new-found convictions. He developed a message that was lucrative for him personally but destructive to the people of God.

There are three warnings from the life of Balaam in the New Testament:

The way of Balaam – 2 Peter 2:15
"They have left the straight way and wandered off to follow the way of Balaam son of Beor, who loved the wages of wickedness."

The way of Balaam is greed and the people that Peter was illustrating by the example of Balaam are described as *"false prophets ... will secretly introduce destructive heresies ... and bring the way of truth into disrepute. In their greed these teachers will exploit you with stories they have made up"* (2 Peter 2:1-3).

The heretics of Peter's day, like Balaam, knew the truth but chose to go a perverse way because of their love of money. Balaam was motivated by material gain and even being rebuked by a donkey did not stop his wickedness. Reader beware, the warning from Balaam underlined by Peter is very relevant for the 21st century church. There are many spiritual charlatans around, ready to fleece God's people with clever stories and attractive teachings.

Balaam's life warns us of the danger of being deceived and used by false prophets. It also calls us to beware of the danger of the love of money which the Bible says is *"a root of all kinds of evil"* (1 Timothy 6:10). Money is a good servant but a very bad master.

The error of Balaam – Jude verse 11

Jude uses strong language to describe the same people that Peter spoke about and his warning is equally severe:

"Woe to them! They have taken the way of Cain; they have rushed for profit into Balaam's error; they have been destroyed in Korah's rebellion."

Jude lists Balaam alongside some of the most disreputable characters in the Old Testament – Cain, the first murderer, and Korah who rebelled against authority so that the earth opened its mouth and swallowed him (see Numbers 16). The "error" of Balaam was that he abandoned the truth in favour of a more lucrative message.

Balaam deliberately deserted the right path in favour of one that led to *"the wages of wickedness."* Three times his donkey, on sighting the angel with the drawn sword, tried to get the prophet off the path he was on, and three times in his determined madness to get his fee for divination, Balaam beat the animal back onto his chosen direction.

The serious error of Balaam was abandoning the right path even when he knew the truth. He knew how essential separation was to Israel's safety but he deliberately used this inside information for personal advantage. His motivation in advising Balak about how to weaken Israel, was his love of money.

The teaching of Balaam – Revelation 2:14

"Nevertheless I have a few things against you: you have people there who hold to the teaching of Balaam, who taught Balak to entice the Israelites to sin by eating food sacrificed to idols and by committing sexual immorality."

In the church at Pergamum, the Nicolaitans had developed a system of belief that compromised their Christian lifestyle. This led to them blending with the world like chameleons so that they would not suffer any persecution for being Christians. This was just what Balaam had taught Balak – how to entice the Israelites to join with the Moabites and Midianites in their idol worship and immorality.

The truth of the gospel is offensive to the world. Living the Christian life as the Bible instructs us will bring us into conflict with the world and its standards, but compromise is not an option for true believers. Three young Hebrew men in the book of Daniel had to choose between bowing to the king's demands, or suffering the penalty of a fiery furnace (Daniel 3). They would not consider compromising.

The way of Balaam was greed – an obsession with money that overruled convictions. The error of Balaam was a rejection of truth in favour of a teaching that won earthly rewards. The teaching of Balaam was compromise – the path of least resistance.

The antidote to Balaam's way of greed is to choose to live generously, using money properly, rejecting the control of materialism and consumerism. The antidote to Balaam's error is to love the truth, holding strongly to its guidance for every area of our lives. The antidote to Balaam's teaching is to reject compromise in all its disguises, choosing rather to live our daily lives with courage and conviction.

Be glad when God says "no" in love. Beware when God says "yes" in anger. Balaam has been dead for a long time, but the warnings from his life are as necessary for today as at any time in the past.

24
Finishing Well

- part one

—⚡︎—

Humpty Dumpty sat on a wall,
Humpty Dumpty had a great fall,
All the king's horses and all the king's men
Couldn't put Humpty together again.

You'll be familiar with the popular nursery rhyme, but in this complicated age some feel the need to ask questions:

"Did Humpty fall or was he pushed? Is this a crime scene or an accident scene? Should Health and Safety be called in to determine whether the wall was safe? Should there have been a notice warning Humpty of danger?" and, "Could the king's men have had a quicker response time to help poor HD?"

A lady once told me that the mistake was to send the king's men; they should have sent the king's women. No comment!

You are probably wondering about the relevance of this discussion!

The point is that there are a lot of Christians who have fallen off the wall that we call church and there are not enough King's men or women to put them back together again.

There are many reasons why people stop going to church, but the overall "fall-out" figures are frightening. Some fall off the wall and others might feel they have been pushed. You could probably think of many former church members yourself – perhaps they used to run well for God but now are far away from God. Some have left church but have not left God – they left to protect their walk with God.

No athlete goes to the Olympics without a plan to win, and in the running of the Christian race we need a sensible plan to enable us to finish well. The outcome has eternal consequences.

Eric Liddell was the Olympian who later went to China as a missionary. He ran to win. In one race he fell – or was he pushed? – and it looked as though he would be last or not finish at all. Yet he picked himself up and ran the race of his life, not just finishing, but winning. A fall, whatever kind and for whatever reason, does not mean you cannot finish well.

In this short study I want us to look at the life of a man in the Bible who started well, ran well and finished well and we will learn some of the essential spiritual factors in his life that ensured his success.

The man we will look at is Philip, the only man in the New Testament who is designated as an evangelist, called "Philip the evangelist." We will look at five windows into the life of this significant man – five basic life principles that profoundly affected his fitness to finish well

(1) Philip growing

In Acts 2:42-47 we get a glimpse of what it was like to be part of the first generation New Testament church. Although Philip is not mentioned by name, it must have been around this time that he became a part of this first congregation.

These early members devoted themselves to four things, and any Christian who wants to finish well must also do the same. The word "devoted" is a strong one; far more than casual attention or intermittent interest, it is a deep commitment to things that contribute to spiritual growth. We each have a personal responsibility for our spiritual health, which means availing ourselves of the right spiritual nourishment. Devotion is done by us, not by someone else for us.

These first Christians "devoted" themselves to four things which assisted their spiritual growth:

• *"The apostles' teaching"*
They loved and were obedient to the teaching of the Word of God. The Old Testament reformer Ezra succeeded because he not only read and studied the Word of God, but he was also dedicated to put it into practice in his own life and then to pass it on to others (Ezra 7:10).

Recent surveys show a serious lack of Bible reading among western Christians. Attendance at conferences, watching God TV and listening to worship CDs are not substitutes for the daily, consistent reading and study of the word of God.

• *"The fellowship"*
In my early Christian days I understood separation as isolation. Since then I have learned that we cannot be salt if we keep hidden in the salt cellar. We need to be in the world (but not of it) to be effective, but we are edified in the place of fellowship. We become like the people we mix with most, so ensure that you find your fellowship with people who will lovingly provoke you to higher living by the lives they live.

• *"The breaking of bread"*
Sometimes called the Lord's Supper, communion, or the Eucharist, this is the occasion when believers gather together to remember

the most basic foundation of the Christian faith – the death and the resurrection of the Lord Jesus. It is sometimes in the context of a shared fellowship meal. This simple act of taking bread and wine (and we are told to do it often) reminds us that no matter how far we progress we owe it all to him. "We are what we are by the grace of God."

• *"Prayer"*
Prayer is both public and private. We need to communicate daily with God, not only to make him aware of our needs, but to enjoy fellowship with him and discover what is on his heart as well.

These four simple, essential spiritual disciplines require our devoted attention, but when practised they lay the foundation to an effective and significant life that will not only run well but also finish well.

Philip will have grown by his devotion to four spiritual disciplines. Before you minister you must mature; before you give out you must take in; and before you bear fruit upwards you must take root downwards.

25
Finishing Well

- part two

—m—

Every Christian wants to finish well. We want to hear the Lord say, "Well done," with no regrets over wasted time or opportunities and the joy of a life lived well for God.

This is more than a dream. It is possible but it will not happen by accident. It will require a dedicated commitment to spiritual health and motivation.

We are looking at the Bible character known as Philip the Evangelist. He started well, ran well and finished well because he built into his life spiritual factors that kept him healthy. He was among that great crowd of Jerusalem's first generation converts who devoted themselves to the four spiritual essentials (Acts 2:42) – teaching from the word (by the apostles), fellowship, prayer and breaking of bread.

Now we look at another spiritual discipline in his life:

(2) Philip serving

Acts 6 describes Jerusalem's first church problem – a dispute about what appeared to be an unfair distribution of help to a vulnerable group of Christians. The Hebrew-speaking widows seemed to be getting more food aid than the Greek-speaking widows. The answer was not for the apostles to work harder but for the burden of church responsibilities to be spread over more workers.

This new ministry would require seven men with the right qualifications *"from among you [church members], known to be full of the Spirit and wisdom."* These high qualifications were not for a high-profile ministry but to serve tables and care for widows. From the thousands of believers in Jerusalem, Philip was an obvious choice, and got overwhelming approval to become one of the seven. So began his ministry of serving in his local church.

Too many Christians are more concerned about being served than serving. They want to be listened to, helped, blessed, ministered to and generally pampered to keep them on board, attending the meetings, and of course giving their tithes. Woe betide the church that doesn't give them what they want, because there are plenty of other churches! This is a sign of spiritual infancy. One of the signs of a mature Christian is the desire and ability to think of the needs of others before their own.

We will see as we progress in this man's life that his faithfulness in serving in basic things allowed God to trust him with greater things. Some are willing to serve but only in the areas that give a platform for their perceived talents. The big question is "Are you willing to volunteer for the basic tasks that get no public fanfare?"

God gets his best conscripts for kingdom work from the ranks of those who serve on tables.

(3) Philip witnessing

Acts 8 shows a dramatic change in Philip's life. After the arrest, trial and martyrdom of Stephen (another table-server), the religious authorities decided it was time to come down hard on these *"people of the way"* (later known as Christians). They found a willing persecutor in a young hate-filled man called Saul of Tarsus (Acts 8:3).

This vicious persecution must have seemed like a tragedy to the Jerusalem members; their exciting church life-style was completely shattered. But what they thought was destruction actually was destiny.

It was eleven years since Pentecost and the church was still in Jerusalem. They had not progressed far in obeying the Great Commission – taking the gospel to Judea, Samaria and the ends of the earth. I am sure they intended to get round to it, but they were taking too long, so God had to step in and break up the comparatively safe and comfortable life-style of the local church.

What will it take to disturb the comfort-zone life-style of most churches in the West?

The believers were scattered and headed for Judea and Samaria (the "ends of the earth" were tackled later through Antioch). Philip headed for Samaria, a marginalised nation of people despised by Jews but not by God. As a Greek-speaking Jew, Philip had learned to minister to Hebrew-speaking widows in Jerusalem. So his cross-cultural ministry skills were put to good use with the Samaritans.

Acts 8:4-8 record the results of the ministry of one man, full of the Holy Ghost and the love and grace of God. He was willing to take a risk and follow the footsteps of his master in going to Samaria (John 4).

The 18th century missionary William Carey was profoundly influenced as a young man by the journals of Captain James Cook. Cook's motto to "go as far as it was possible for a man to go" challenged him. Carey determined to go as far as possible for God and Carey's motto became "Attempt great things for God. Expect great things from God."

Philip, the server of tables, attempted great things for God and saw great things from God. The whole city was filled with great joy.

If you want to finish well, keep witnessing. Philip turned a city the right way up by just telling the truth about Jesus. We are all called to be witnesses for Christ and we are whether we like it or not – either good ones or bad ones. To be a witness you don't have to be a theologian or able to answer all questions – just tell the truth about Jesus and what he has done in your life.

Your story of God's dealings in your life is unique, like other things belonging to you alone – your fingerprints, your DNA and your heart rhythm. The apostle Paul was a great theologian and had "out-of-this-world" experiences, yet he loved to give his testimony.

Keep growing, keep serving and keep witnessing – they all contribute to "finishing well."

26

Finishing Well

- part three

—ᴍ—

Michael Phelps won eight gold medals at the 2008 Beijing Olympics, making him the most successful athlete of the games. His whole lifestyle was dedicated to being at peak performance for the games, so no aspect of his life was overlooked. He had high goals.

Philip was a man in the New Testament who set high goals and achieved them – he started well, ran well and finished well. We are taking note of the disciplines that he built into his life to be a winner – he was committed to continuous spiritual growth, he learned to serve in his local church, and he took risks in witnessing for Christ.

Now we look at two final factors of his significant life:

(4) Philip obedient

We have already seen that Philip was involved in a great revival in Samaria. The whole city was full of joy, many were saved, healed and delivered, and then two Jerusalem apostles visited and prayed for the converts to receive a powerful baptism in the Holy Ghost. It was exciting and fulfilling.

But suddenly there was a major interruption:

"Now an angel of the Lord said to Philip, 'Go south to the road – the desert road – that goes from Jerusalem to Judea. So he started out..." (Acts 8:26-27)

Many people hear God when he says, "Leave the desert and go to the revival," but not so many hear him when he says, "Leave the revival and go to the desert."

Philip's instant obedience is impressive, with no arguments about delaying this request or doubts about what he could possibly do for God in the desert. His prompt obedience put him in the right place at the right time to meet a very significant person – the Chancellor of the Exchequer for country of Ethiopia.

The timing of God is as important as the will of God, and the man's conversion had repercussions for a nation. This royal official had been to Jerusalem to worship but was returning unsatisfied, and as part of his search for God he had purchased (at great expense) a scroll containing the book of Isaiah. He would probably have been travelling with a significant number of people, including soldiers, other officials and servants.

God had taken Philip, a table server turned evangelist, out of a revival in Samaria down into a dry desert. Because of his obedience, he was in the right place to hear the man read aloud from Isaiah's prophecy about the sufferings of Christ. At the Ethiopian's invitation, Philip got up into the chariot and beginning at the same scripture passage, gave him the good news of Jesus.

In front of all his servants, soldiers and officials the man requested baptism in a desert pool. Baptismal services don't get any more exciting than this. But that is not the end of the surprises:

"When they came up out of the water, the Spirit of the Lord suddenly took Philip away, and the eunuch did not see him again, but went on his way rejoicing. Philip, however, appeared at Azotus and travelled about preaching the gospel in all the towns."

Philip's obedience opened up a lot of dramatic ministry – a revival in Samaria, an angelic message, witnessing to a high Royal Official and baptising him in water. And then there was Holy Ghost transport to a new ministry in Azotus, among Israel's ancient enemies, the Philistines. This brings us to the last picture of Philip:

(5) – Philip faithful

Acts 8:40 closes as Philip reaches Caesarea and we have to turn to Acts 21:8 to meet him again. He is still in Caesarea, and once again serves tables as he entertains Paul and his travel companions who were on their way to Jerusalem. His life was less dramatic and more settled, but he was still serving.

A lot can happen in twenty years, and it appears that Philip is now a married man with four daughters. Now for a Jewish man to have no sons was regarded as a tragedy but however disappointing this might have been for Philip, he was still being spiritually fruitful – his daughters prophesied.

As you will see from Acts 21, prophecy featured quite highly at this time in Paul's life. In the home of Philip the Evangelist, Paul received ministry to help prepare him for the big challenge that lay ahead for him in Jerusalem.

Philip had been privileged to be used by God in some quite dramatic ways. He now had a less spectacular life as a husband, father and householder, but was living just as faithfully for God. Some think they are only pleasing God when they are doing sensational things, but faithfulness in the mundane is just as pleasing to God – *"Well done, good and **faithful** servant."*

So, what have we learned from this man who started well, ran well and finished well?

The five pictures we get of him underline five basic spiritual life principles that are essential for spiritual health: keep growing, keep serving, keep witnessing, keep obedient and keep faithful in every season of life. As we persevere in these disciplines they will help us to "finish well."

27

The Fellowship of the Limp

- part one

—m—

The story we are going to look at has all the ingredients of a Hollywood epic – family tensions, simmering hatred, sibling rivalry, threats of murder and extreme jealousy but it also has romance, unusual courting and marriage rituals, and polygamy. The dramatic climax – the reason for the title – has one of the most amazing encounters in the Bible.

The story opens in Genesis 25 with a very pregnant and very perplexed lady, Rebekah. This is the first recorded incident in the Bible of someone carrying twins, and she is concerned about the unusual sensation of two babies struggling in her womb. She asked God a question that I think many women about to give birth have also asked: "Why is this happening to me?"

A 1988 film called "Twins" featured Arnold Schwarzenegger and Danny DeVito, who though supposed to be twins, were not identical or even slightly alike. The twins born to Isaac's wife Rebekah that day also were not identical; the first to be born was Esau and the Bible describes him as red and like a hairy garment. The second was born grasping his brother's heel and so was called Jacob, "the grasper." What he was by name he was by nature.

So many ingredients go into the shaping of a person's personality. As we look at the life and makeup of Jacob, you may catch a glimpse of yourself, but persevere to the end of the story because despite a bad start, Jacob ended up well.

God sometimes refers to himself as the God of Abraham, Isaac and Jacob: quite a significant accolade for a man who started off being called "the grasper." The Bible is full of illustrations of how God can take flawed material and turn them into significant people. This is one such story.

I would like to present several factors from the life of Jacob that can powerfully affect how a person turns out.

What Jacob was by birth

Esau and Jacob were very different physically but the distinction did not end there. Jacob is described as a "quiet man," smooth skinned and one who liked to stay among the tents indulging in his hobby, cooking, which, in those days was very much women's work. He was his mother's favourite.

Esau, on the other hand, was a rugged outdoor pursuits type who liked the open skies and hunting. He was a man's man, and nobody kicked sand in his face! He was his father's favourite and both enjoyed time together after a hunt eating some of Esau's freshly caught meat together.

Some people are advantaged from birth. Maybe they have a well-off family, good physical attributes, a sharp brain, a likeable personality or a great sense of humour that makes them very popular with others. Others may struggle from the moment they are born with poverty, plain looks, limited opportunities or the shadow of a successful sibling. Some fail to rise to the expectations of parents and permanently feel like a failure.

Jacob may have had a difficult start growing up under the shadow of a very confident and popular brother, but as we will see, how he turned out in the end is what really matters.

Some people compare themselves with others, imagining that other people appear to have everything going their way. Perhaps in their hearts they ask why God seems to have given others so much and them so little. Romans 9:20 warns against this: *"Shall what is formed say to him who formed it, 'Why did you make me like this?'"* Psalm 139 reminds us that the Creator put personal thought into every person which makes us all unique and of special value.

What Jacob became by the influence of other people

We are all influenced by other people, and Jacob, who was close to his mother, was very much affected by her ambitions for him.

To Jacob, two things were of great importance – the birthright and the blessing, both of which belonged to the first-born who was Esau. However his mother had communicated to him the promise God had given her before the twins were born – that the elder would serve the younger, a reversal of the normal order. So without waiting for God to bring it about, mother and son devised their own ways of making it happen.

The transfer of the birthright was almost too easy. Jacob took advantage of his brother's hunger after he came home from a hunt and demanded his transfer of the birthright in exchange for a bowl of red lentil stew. Esau placed no value on this very spiritual thing, whereas Jacob put a high value on it.
The Bible declares that Esau despised his birthright.

The transfer of the blessing was more difficult and required the direct involvement of his mother and a very dangerous game of dressing up. The next chapter will explore this event further as well as other lessons from Jacob's life.

28

The Fellowship of the Limp

- part two

—ɯ—

Jacob was grasping bigger things than Esau's heel now. He had deceived his brother into surrendering the birthright, and was now scheming with his mother about how to deceive the father and his brother over the blessing.

A father's blessing, especially on his first-born son, is powerful because it carries the authority of heaven behind it. Fathers should remember that God has delegated authority to them. That loving authority expressed in their words and prayers can have a powerful effect on their children.

We are looking at the life-shaping influences that go into the making of a person. So far we have seen how much birth can affect a person and then we started on the influence that other people can have on us:

What Jacob became by the influence of his mother

Rebekah remembered the prophecy that the older would serve the younger. She was determined to see it happen, even if it meant resorting to deception and lies. It's commendable to have good ambitions but the way we achieve them is also important.

Genesis 27 is a sad chapter of a family divided by deception, lies and pretence. It starts with Isaac asking Esau to prepare a meal so that he can enjoy it and then confer his final blessing on his eldest son. Rebekah overheard the conversation and decided it was her favourite son, Jacob, who should get in first. They hatched a duplicitous plan which involved Jacob dressing as his brother, even to covering his arms with goat hair and then going into his father to dupe him into conferring the blessing on him and not on Esau.

The deception worked, and Jacob was hardly out of the tent before Esau arrived. On discovering Jacob's theft of the blessing, he threatened to kill his brother after his father's death. Despite Esau's tearful pleading with his father for the blessing to be redirected to him, he finally realised that his spiritual carelessness had a very high price (see Hebrews 12:17). Jacob left home in a hurry to stay with his uncle Laban until Esau, hopefully, would have cooled off.

Rebekah's influence with Jacob's collusion resulted in a very deep family divide, both in the short and long term. To this day animosity remains between the descendents of Esau (the Arab nations) and the descendents of Jacob (the nation of Israel).

There is no doubt that other people can have a very powerful influence in shaping a person's life. Words, actions, pressure, neglect, and criticism, especially when dispensed by those close, can negatively affect development. In some situations they can leave someone emotionally crippled for life

What Jacob became by personal mistakes and choices

It's not just birth and the behaviour of others that affect the kind of people we become. We also have a responsibility for the decisions or mistakes we make, and they also can leave a long-lasting legacy in our lives.

Genesis 27 closes with Jacob fleeing from the murderous threats of his brother. He ended up staying with his uncle Laban who also turned out to be a consummate deceiver. But even Laban had something to learn about deception from Jacob.

In Genesis 29 Jacob fell in love with Rachel but was deceived into marrying her sister Leah first. The whole exercise cost him 14 years of unpaid employment, but because he was so much in love with Rachel, they only seemed like days to him. Knowing the character of Jacob it's hard to see him in the role of star-struck lover!

The deceiver had been well and truly deceived by Laban but then he began a series of cunning business enterprises that virtually stripped his uncle of all his flocks and herds. Jacob ended up a very wealthy man, but the cost was more simmering family hatred. The sons of Laban complained, *"Jacob has taken everything our father owned and has gained all this wealth from what belonged to our father"* (Genesis 31:1).

Jacob was smart enough to realise that once more the atmosphere in the family towards him was not positive. It was time to leave, and the rest of Genesis 31 records a very fraught family parting. The result was that God warned Laban in a dream that he should be careful not to take revenge on his son-in-law.

The tense meeting with Laban and Jacob finishes up with what has been called the Mizpah blessing, *"May the Lord keep watch between you and me when we are away from each other"* (Genesis 31:49). Despite the lovely-sounding sentiments, it was a strong warning and threat for neither party to cross that boundary to harm the other – God was the witness, he was watching!

Jacob was now greatly enriched with flocks and herds and many servants, as well as two wives and 12 children. But the price of his grasping materialism had been high. He was now estranged from his own family and from his wives' family, leaving a trail of hurt and broken relationships behind him.

So far we have seen how birth, other people, and his own decisions and mistakes had powerfully shaped Jacob's life. As you look at Jacob's life, you may even see a reflection of some aspects of your own life. I am so glad that the story does not stop there!

As we look deeper at the life of Jacob, we see that the Almighty God had been providentially moving in the background. Despite Jacob's failings, God was at work in the life of Jacob in dreams, angelic visitations and behind-the-scenes protection. He was moving up to one of the most amazing God encounters in the entire Bible. The grasper was about to meet the God of grace.

29
The Fellowship of the Limp

- part three

—⚍—

Powerful factors had contributed to the shaping of Jacob – what he was by birth, what he became by the influence of his mother and also what he became by his own decisions and choices. But that was not the end of the story.

God had plans for the life of this grasper who always got what he wanted, often by deception. Despite his obvious materialistic success, he was isolated and disliked, but little did Jacob realise that the plan of God was coming to a climax.

The Fellowship of the Limp is an unofficial fellowship of people who have come to a point in their walk with God that has involved a serious breaking experience. The staff of self confidence is broken and replaced with a total dependence on God's power. Jacob was the founder member of this fellowship and his breaking experience left him with a permanent limp. We now come to the last and most important feature in the turning of a Jacob into Israel:

What Jacob became by his encounter with God

After the threats from his father-in-law, Jacob decided it was time to make contact with his brother Esau. He sent a messenger to tell Esau that he was on his way to meet him. The messenger returned with the news that Esau was on his way to meet Jacob accompanied by 400 trained servants. This could only mean one thing – Esau was coming to fulfil his promise to kill Jacob.

The Bible describes Jacob's reaction: *"great fear and distress"* (Genesis 32:7). He began to pray, passionately reminding God of his promises to him and asking for protection. Life's crises are usually good motivators for prayer.

Unsurprisingly, as well as praying, the scheming mind of this sharp business man kicked into overdrive and he devised plans that he hoped would soften his brother's angry intentions. These plans involved generous presents sent on ahead for his brother, followed by all his remaining possessions. Then his wives and children were divided into two groups and also sent on an interception course with Esau.

After all this was done, Jacob was left alone in his camp contemplating the meeting the next day with his brother (Genesis 32:24). As he sat, deep in fearful thought, he became aware of the presence of another man in his camp. Jacob was unaware of his unexpected visitor's identity, but we know that this was God in a human form (a theophany).

We then have the astounding record of God physically wrestling with a man who was known as a grasper and a deceiver. This was not just a short bout that was quickly over; this contest went on for the whole night.

Wrestling is not a genteel sport. It is very physical, sweaty and close contact.

Finally when God saw that his opponent would not give in, he abandoned humanity and resorted to a little divinity: *"When the man saw that he could not overpower him, he touched the socket of Jacob's hip."* Amazingly, as the dawn broke God announced to Jacob that he had won – *"You have struggled with God and with men and have overcome."*

As Jacob limped away from Peniel and faced the dawn of a new day, he was a much poorer man (Esau kept all the gifts) but a man with a new name, Israel, a new nature and a new walk. Every step after this encounter was a reminder that it was the living God who had struggled with him and changed his life. He said, *"I saw God face to face, and yet my life was spared."*

Genesis 32 is well worth an unhurried read. It could be very significant for you. As I read this story, three words stand out strongly and seem to sum up the drama:

1. Deception – this sums up the old Jacob, what he was by birth, what he became by his mother's influence and also by his own choices and mistakes. He was a man who got what he wanted and didn't stop too much to examine the way he got them.

2. Struggle – God summed up his life thus far – "You have struggled with men and have overcome". Right from the womb he had struggled – with his brother, his father-in-law and his whole family. Yes, he usually came out on top, but the price in human relationships was very high.

3. Overcoming – As Jacob wrestled with his Maker, God must have been delighted at the determination of this man not to let him go until he was blessed. God loves spiritually persistent people. Some struggle with God but don't persevere through to victory.

This physical wrestling match seems to be a one-off. Yet the fact that it lasted the whole night suggests that God enjoyed turning a deceiving grasper into a new man called Israel. God is still in the same business.

Jacob's new name also became the name for the emerging nation, Israel. What was true of Jacob has also been true of the nation. Their history has been one of struggling with others for survival and also struggling with God, summed up in their rejection of Christ the Messiah.

People are initiated into the fellowship of the limp in many different ways, but there are similar ingredients. First there is an experience that cannot be solved by human ability, followed by a period of struggle that requires spiritual persistence. This then leads to a different way of living that rejects human strength and ability in favour of total dependence on God.

The breaking experience of Jacob is still happening today. Our God of incredible love and grace still delights in getting personally involved in the messed-up lives of modern day Jacobs, and turning them into exhibits of his power to change.

Jacob's meeting with his brother went well, they wept and embraced and there was no killing. The whole story can be read in Genesis chapter 33. But take note of verse 16 which suggests that Jacobs's old deceiving nature wasn't totally eradicated at his wrestling match with God! We can all identify with that.

30

From Useful to Useless and Back Again

—⟶—

Have you ever felt like running away? When the pressures and responsibilities of life seem overwhelming, the grass on the other side of the fence definitely looks greener and the temptation for a change of scenery is strong. I once saw a baby's bib that said, "That's it! I'm off to Grandma's."

In one of the smallest books of the Bible, there is a gem of a story about a young man who ran away. At first it seemed the answer to his problems, but that soon changed and he ended up in prison where he found a lasting answer to his empty heart.

The story is wrapped up in the very short letter of Paul to Philemon; it would only take you a few minutes to read the story for yourself. You have to use a detective's mind to piece it all together but it appears to have happened like this:

There was a young slave by the name of Onesimus who lived in the city of Colossae. He felt there was a big world out there for him to explore and so he stole some money from his master and took off for the bright lights of Rome. No doubt he had lots of friends when he had money, but they disappeared like the morning mist when the money ran out and he needed help.

He seems to have been sent to prison where he met a rather beat-up old man called Paul along with quite a few of his companions. When Paul introduced him to Christ, his life was turned around and he became like a son to Paul.

But now he and Paul were faced with a problem. Onesimus was a fugitive and a thief and the right thing to do was to go back to his master and "face the music." The punishment for running away was branding, but for stealing it could be death. What should he do?

Christ's forgiveness of our sins does not absolve us from the consequences of breaking the law, even bad laws. The Holy Spirit will give us the power to do what is right, not just what is convenient or easy. As Paul and Onesimus talked, they discovered that Paul knew his master, a man called Philemon in whose house the Colossian church met. It also turned out that Paul had just written a letter to the church at Colossae which was about to be hand-delivered by Tychicus, one of Paul's companions.

It was decided that Philemon should accompany this man back to Colossae carrying a personal letter from Paul to Philemon pleading for the life of the newly born-again runaway. This is the letter in your Bible called Philemon which is squeezed in between Titus and Hebrews. Perhaps you will read it with different eyes now! The letter is highly illuminating.

Paul describes Philemon

This good friend and good worker was remarkable for:

• His faith in Christ and his love for all the saints, the two irreducible elements of the Christian life

• His generosity – another translation of verse 6 is *"Your habit of generously sharing all you have with others will lead you more deeply into the knowledge of the good things in Christ."* The more we open our hands to minister to others, the more we open our hearts for God to minister to us. The more like Christ we become, the more generous we will be to others.

• His practical love for Christians. He was rich and generous – a rare combination.

Paul pleads for Onesimus

Using much wisdom in compiling the letter, Paul doesn't command Philemon; he asks him for a big favour. He asks his friend to rise above the normal master/slave relationship and see the bigger miracle that was happening. The gospel was completely overturning old lines of division between Jews and Gentiles, slaves and free, and male and female.

Because of Christ the relationship had changed – Onesimus left as a slave and a thief. He was returning still as a slave but also now a brother. The gospel has the power to change deeply embedded mindsets and long-standing cultural divisions. Paul pleads as an advocate for the life of a man who cannot defend himself (compare 1 John 2:1). He does not make excuses for Onesimus, but pleads on the basis of a changed relationship.

The name Onesimus means "useful" but because of sin he became "useless"; however thanks to Christ he once more became "useful." Only God can make the useless useful and he calls us to partner with him in this work of restoring "useless" people

William Barclay gives an interesting postscript to this story. Fifty years later, a Christian leader called Ignatius was on his way to Rome as a prisoner to be executed. At points along the journey he wrote letters to the nearby churches. When he stopped at Smyrna he wrote a letter to the church at Ephesus with a lot of good things to say about the leader of the church, a man called Onesimus.

Could it be that the runaway slave had become the leader of one of the foremost churches in the New Testament? If so, then Philemon had done what Paul had asked for and Onesimus had become one of Paul's trusted workers. The useless one had become a very useful one. God has chosen the weak, foolish and despised things of this world, and in the first century Roman Empire, what could be more weak, foolish or despised than a slave? This has the fingerprints of God all over it.

31
The Secret Miracle

- part one

—⟋⟋—

In John chapter 2 we have the very first miracle of Jesus, the turning of water into wine. As a lifelong teetotaller, I must confess that this first miracle leaves me with some questions. After all, Jesus turned 180 gallons (almost 820 litres) of ordinary well water into 180 gallons of high quality wine – a small wine lake! Why didn't he choose something different for his first miracle?

Now I know that Jesus was not encouraging drunkenness. So apart from helping a newly married young couple out of a problem, what was the point of this miracle?

When I read the Bible I always try to look for the story behind the story, the human interest application that will help us know Christ better and live better.

The Bible is full of stories about people – how they coped with life, conquered their difficulties, got on with awkward people and advanced in their walk with God, especially when he wasn't doing things their way.

John refers to the miracles of Jesus as *signs*. A sign is never an end in itself; it always points to something more important. For example, the burning bush was a sign to get Moses' attention but when he turned aside to see it, he forgot the sign in the importance of listening to what God had to say.

John, in his Gospel, records eight miracles or signs that Jesus performed. While the signs are mighty, they point to something bigger than the miracle. They lift the mind from the physical to the spiritual.

One of the first things that struck me was the fact that very few people would be aware that a miracle had taken place. That's why I call it "the secret miracle," or, "The wedding crisis that few were aware of."

First-century Jewish weddings could last for up to a week. After the initial ceremony and the wedding feast, the couple would be led in a torch-lit procession through the streets to their new home. This was not to enjoy a quiet and private honeymoon, but to hold open house for several days with the bride wearing her wedding dress. So the matter of hospitality was an important one.

The wine running out was more than a mere inconvenience; it would cause the young couple and their parents great embarrassment and humiliation. Was it caused by bad planning or was it the presence of some unexpected guests (Jesus and five disciples for example)?

Whatever the cause, Mary, the mother of Jesus, obviously had an important role to play in the solving of the problem. She instinctively went to Jesus. His reply to her request for help seems like a rebuke, but she clearly did not take it as such.

It's clear that Jesus would not act to anyone else's agenda or timetable, even his mother's – *"Dear lady, let me handle this in my own way,"* is one translation of his reply. Perhaps he hesitated, aware that the moment this first miracle happened he would be crossing a line with no going back. This miracle and the ones to follow set him on the course leading up to "his hour" of crucifixion.

Whatever the reason Jesus gave this reply, it obviously did not put Mary off, because her simple command to the servants was, *"Do whatever he tells you"*(John 2:5).

The six stone water jars were used for ritual cleansing – the washing of feet and hands. They could contain up to 180 gallons of water, so to fill them to the brim would be very hard work for the servants, requiring scores of trips to the well. I wonder if they were tempted to think, "We need more wine, not more water, so why are we doing this?" Then, when they were commanded to dip their pitchers in the "water" and take it to the guests, their faith and obedience was really stretched.

I wonder when the well water turned into high quality wine. But whenever the miracle happened, the master of ceremonies at the wedding had no doubts about the quality of what he tasted. It was obviously a well-known practice for the good stuff to be brought out at the beginning and the cheaper stuff when the guests had drunk a lot, but at this wedding the best had been kept to the last.

What does this "sign" teach us?
"This was the first miracle that Jesus performed and was part of the foundation of his forthcoming ministry."

Beginnings are important in setting the tone and values of what would follow, so what does this first sign of Jesus point to regarding the kind of ministry that would follow?

It was the first manifestation of his glory – verse 11
This, the first of the miraculous signs, Jesus performed at Cana in Galilee. He thus revealed his glory, and his disciples put their faith in him.

Some might say "What a waste of a miracle!" Hardly anyone was aware it had happened, and it wasn't a miracle of healing or deliverance. It was a miracle of supply and hardly the supply of something vital – just more wine for people who had probably already drunk quite a lot.

This was the first miracle for hundreds of years. The four hundred years between Malachi and Matthew was a period of spiritual dryness – no voice from God, no signs and no miracles. Yet this miracle of Jesus was done quietly. Imagine if Saatchi and Saatchi or some government spin doctors had been given the contract to plan the launch of his miracle ministry. It would not have been a secret miracle; they would have planned for something more spectacular.

32

The Secret Miracle

- part two

—⁂—

The first miracle of Jesus at a wedding in Cana set the tone for his ministry which was just beginning. It was the first glimpse of his glory that his disciples got.

Jesus had a ministry of generosity

The supply wasn't just enough to meet the need. It was superabundance, over-the-top generosity, lavish giving. This certainly was a sign of the forthcoming ministry of Jesus – abundant mercy and grace, total forgiveness and joyful generosity.

This remarkable supply would later be seen in the feeding of five thousand men plus women and children, with each one having all they wanted and more than twelve baskets left over. All from five loaves and a few fishes!

When God made the world, he built in fruitfulness to abundantly meet every need. When God fed a large nation in the wilderness, for forty years there was a daily provision for the needs of every person, along with a lavish supply of water from a rock. In addition, there was heat, light and shade from the cloud that led them.

The message or the sign is clear; Jesus came to reveal the generous heart of God. Paul's opening prayer in Ephesians chapter 1:7-8 speaks of *"the riches of God's grace that he lavished on us with all wisdom and understanding."*

Jesus doesn't sensationalise the supernatural

There was no fanfare of trumpets for this, his first miracle; no attempt to impress or dazzle people. There was a reserve in the way Jesus met this need and manifested his glory. Philip Yancey refers to it as divine shyness and says, "No pyrotechnic display of divine omnipotence will achieve the response God desires."

Seven times in Mark's gospel, Jesus instructs people who have been healed, "Tell no one." The greatest display of divine power was the resurrection, yet no one saw it happen. No one was there when Jesus emerged through the funeral bandages or when the angel pushed the stone aside. To meet the person who is the resurrection is more important than witnessing the event.

We love the dramatic and the exciting, but they seldom make good converts. People who are attracted only by the sensational will expect to be kept by increasingly sensational acts.

Jesus loved to be with ordinary people

Jesus did not gravitate to the good and the great; he was not impressed with fame or title. He could be very much at home at feasts, celebrations and weddings. It even got him the undeserved reputation of being a drunk and a glutton. Jesus had some "unsavoury" friends – tax collectors, sinners, prostitutes and others from the underbelly of society called him friend.

Jesus never went soft on sin but people who felt bad about themselves felt comfortable being around Jesus. The first miracle took place at the wedding of an un-named peasant couple in a rather obscure village with hardly anyone aware of it actually happening. What a challenge to the climate of forced hype we often find in many churches today.

Jesus can take the ordinary and make it extraordinary

Water from a well, used for ritual washing of hands and feet turned into something praised by a connoisseur of wedding wine. It was a sign that the water of the Law was being turned into the new wine of the joy of God's kingdom.

Jesus loves to take the basic stuff of life and make it shine with the glory of his presence. He is as much with us in the ordinary routine as he is in the dramatic times. Psalm 23 reminds us that the Good Shepherd is with us by the quiet waters, in the green pastures, in the valley of the shadow of death, preparing a table in the presence of danger, in fact all the way till we "dwell in the house of the Lord for ever."

So this sign pointed to these defining characteristics of the forthcoming ministry of Jesus:

- It would be astonishingly generous.
- It would be supernatural without being sensational. Jesus would never turn the meeting of human need into a media event.
- It would focus on people from all walks of life regardless of their status, position or title.
- It would delight in invading ordinary life with displays of God's generous grace.

There are two more life lessons we can glean from this first sign:

Disciples and servants see more than guests

The only people who were immediately aware that a miracle had taken place were the disciples and the servants. The guests, the young couple and the parents all got the benefit but only the disciples and the servants saw his glory.

They were the ones who put in the hard work to fill the six jars. They exercised faith when commanded to draw out the supposed water and take the risk in presenting it to the guests as wine. Jesus told them to fill the jars but the servants "filled them to the brim" – they went the extra mile and gave Jesus plenty of raw materials to work with. Participants will always see more than spectators.

How do you cope when the supply runs out?

"The wine has run out."

This could have brought the whole event to an embarrassing end and ruined the couple's special day, but they had made the wise decision to invite Jesus!

The "wine" can run out in a marriage, when the love, respect and pleasure dries up and all that is left is a union in name only.

The "wine" can run out in church life – when the enjoyment, anticipation and pleasure of being together gives way to boring ritual, predictable meetings, going through the motions, formality and rules.

The "wine" can run out in a Christian's personal experience – when spiritual ambition, faith, joy and excitement give way to criticism, cynicism, unreality and reluctance to be involved.

The wine ran out at the wedding in Cana but Mary did the right thing – she took the matter to Jesus and asked him to become involved.

Many of us love to receive neatly packaged prophetic words in a prayer line, accompanied by dramatic displays of power. But sometimes the longer lasting answers come in an unspectacular way through "secret" miracles and private encounters with Christ.

33
The Set of the Sails

- part one

—∽⁓—

A W Tozer was a well respected preacher from the first half of the 20th century. He was also a prolific writer of over forty book and numerous articles. One editorial he wrote was entitled 'The Set of the Sails' and it started with this poem:

> One ship drives east and another drives west
> With the selfsame wind that blows
> It's the set of the sails and not the gales
> Which tell us the way to go.

By adjusting his sail, a sailor can make any wind, even a contrary one, work for him and take him in the direction he wants to go.

Whoever wrote this sentence caught a great truth: "Whatever captures your heart will control your life and determine your destiny." This agrees with the proverb, *"Above all else, guard your heart, for it is the wellspring of life"* (Proverbs 4:23).

This lesson will focus on a man who, despite the prevailing violence and corruption of his day, put a permanent guard on his heart. To find this man we have to go back to the very beginning of recorded time. Adam was still alive, people were multiplying on the face of the earth but, sadly, sin, corruption and violence were also spreading like a plague. I am sure the contemporaries of Adam must have plied him with many questions about what life was like in the Garden of Eden before sin got him expelled.

The man we are going to learn from is Enoch, about whom the Bible simply says, "He walked with God." The Bible very succinctly sums up what we need to know about him in seven verses. Here are five of them:

"When Enoch had lived 65 years, he became the father of Methuselah. After he became the father of Methuselah, Enoch walked with God for 300 years and had other sons and daughters. Altogether, Enoch lived 365 years. Enoch walked with God; then he was no more, because God took him away." (Genesis 5:21-24)

"By faith Enoch was taken away from this life, so that he did not experience death; he could not be found, because God had taken him away. For before he was taken, he was commended as one who pleased God." (Hebrews 11:5)

Later we will read what the book of Jude says about him, but even all seven verses put together make only a fraction of a page. It is a very brief summary, especially when you consider that some modern biographies can run to hundreds of pages. Nevertheless, what we read tells us that there are lessons to be learned from this man. Let's gather up some of the facts so far:

He lived like his contemporaries for the first 65 years of his life. He followed the pattern of those who had gone before him, an unremarkable and uneventful first 65 years.

He changed when his son Methuselah was born. He no longer just "lived," he broke the treadmill of existence and from that time on began to walk with God. He maintained this walk for 300 years.

He had a revelation that affected how he viewed the world he lived in. He called his son, Methuselah: "When he is dead, it shall come." Methuselah died the year of the flood. We will see more of this shortly from the book of Jude.

He walked with God for 300 years, in such a way that he was commended by God. This walk with God would affect every part of his daily life.

He had faith because it was by faith he was removed from this earth.

He did not die. People must have looked for him when he failed to come home, but he could not be found because God had taken him. Enoch was one of only two men in the Bible who did not die. The other one was Elijah who was caught up to heaven in a whirlwind (2 Kings 2).

Enoch had a life-affecting revelation

Today we have information overload and revelation deficit. I find that God seldom explains himself, but instead gives revelation. There is a day coming when every question will be answered, but for the moment we live by faith in the character and justice of God.

At the end of the book of Job, after Job had bombarded a silent heaven with questions about his situation, God finally spoke out of a storm. Yet instead of addressing Job's painful circumstances or answering his questions, God gave Job a revelation.

God plied Job with scores of questions about the natural world, none of which he was able to answer. Finally Job covered his mouth, admitted that he spoke out of ignorance (Job 42:1-6) and confessed, *"My ears have heard of you but now my eyes have seen you. Therefore I despise myself and repent in dust and ashes."* Job was healed of his grief and changed for the rest of his life – not by explanations, but by revelation.

Enoch had a revelation about the coming judgment of God on a world mired in violence and corruption. Listen to the description of the condition of the world that Enoch lived in:

"The Lord saw how great man's wickedness on the earth had become and that every inclination of the thoughts of his heart was only evil all the time. The Lord was grieved that he had made man on the earth and his heart was filled with pain...

... Now the earth was corrupt in God's sight and was full of violence. God saw how corrupt the earth had become, for all the people on earth had corrupted their ways." (Genesis 6:5-6, 11-12)

Genesis 6 also shows us the breakdown between the separation of the godly line of Seth and the ungodly line of Cain. The consequence was that God set a deadline of 120 years before the judgment of the flood would come.

Into this corrupt and violent atmosphere Methuselah was born. The birth of his son, accompanied by the revelation he received from God concerning the future, changed the way Enoch lived the rest of his life. He made a definite choice that from that moment on he would walk with God, regardless of what others might do.

In the book of Jude we will look more closely at the life-affecting revelation that Enoch had, and the difference it could make in our lives.

34
The Set of the Sails

- part two

—◦◦◦—

For most people the birth of a child is a life-changing experience. It's a sobering fact that the child is likely to demand your time, energy and resources for the next 20 years of your life.

Enoch was affected by the birth of his son Methuselah and it changed him from a man who just "lived" to a man who walked with God. This lasted for the next 300 years of his life. At the same time he also received a revelation from God about the coming judgment of God on a corrupt and evil world.

Jude records his revelation:

"Enoch, the seventh from Adam, prophesied about these men: 'See, the Lord is coming with thousands upon thousands of his holy ones to judge everyone, and to convict all the ungodly of the ungodly acts they have done in the ungodly way, and all the harsh words ungodly sinners have spoken against him.'" (Jude 14-15)

Jude (probably the brother of Jesus) set out to write a comforting letter about our shared salvation. He was so troubled by current events in the church, however, that he changed his subject to a much sterner one – the judgment of God.

Jude was concerned about the fact that the church of his day was being undermined and invaded by teachers who made the grace of God a licence for immorality (Jude 4). As part of his warning, he quoted those words of Enoch.

Both Jude and Enoch were concerned that wickedness was invading the people of God, blurring the lines of distinction between God's people and the world. If that warning was true in the days of Jude and Enoch, how much more is it today? Jesus did warn us (Matthew 24:12) that, *"Because of the increase of wickedness, the love of most will grow cold."*

Like most Christians I prefer to focus on the grace and the mercy of God. But it must be balanced with the truth of God's coming judgment on sin. If the violence of Enoch's day attracted the sternness of God, how much more will this be the case in our generation?

Enoch's walk with God

Enoch is recorded as one of the heroes in the Hebrews 11 hall of faith. However, he is not mentioned because of a great deed or exceptional courage. While others in Hebrews 11 were famous for walking through fire, sleeping unharmed with lions or seeing their dead brought back to life, Enoch's contribution was that he "walked with God." Despite the prevailing winds of his day he set his sail to go in God's direction.

Let me mention four features of Enoch's walk with God:

1. It had a start. He didn't just drift into it, and it was not something God or anyone else did for him. He made a definite and personal choice when his son was born to begin a walk with God.

2. It was genuine enough to stand the test of the remaining 300 years of his life. It is one thing to be emotionally moved on a Sunday, go to the front and make a commitment, but the reality is tested by the decision that is made on a Monday morning. We need to be just as determined to follow God in the narrow groove of everyday life.

3. It was consistent. It was a walk, not a 100-metre dash or a hop, skip or jump. The picture of a walk suggests something that is steady, paced and reliable.

4. It carried a reward: God took him away to his home. The same will happen at a set day in the future when believers who, like Enoch, have consistently walked with God will be "caught up' to walk with God in his place (see 1 Thessalonians 4:13-18).

"What captures your heart controls your life and will determine your destiny." The question needs to be asked, "Has your heart been captured to serve God and walk with him?" The psalmist David said, *"My heart is steadfast, O God, my heart is steadfast"* (Psalm 57:7).

There are many reasons why some people stop walking with God. For some it is because God has not responded or helped them in the way they expected, and they become bitter and angry. Others, like Demas, are lured away by the deceitfulness of riches; materialism is a powerful weapon used by Satan against the saints. Still others get their eyes off the Lord and onto other things or people.

Yes, we have a determined foe but with the whole armour of God, the word of God and the Spirit of God, there is no need for our walk to be interrupted. It's the set of our sails and not the gales that determine the way we go. Even contrary winds can be used for our benefit and the advancement of the kingdom of God.

I've known my friend, Andy McHolm, for over 60 years. He was brought up in the country and so knows a lot about nature. Some years ago he and I were walking in a forest after a severe storm, and came across a tree that had been blown over. Andy pointed out that this one had fallen when the others around it had not, because it had no deep roots, only shallow ones. The shallow roots were sufficient in normal conditions but could not handle a bad storm.

Storms come to all believers, but the "set of your sail" will determine whether or not the storm works for or against you. Enoch lived at a time when a major storm of corruption, wickedness and violence was engulfing the whole of mankind but he had "set his sail" to walk with God regardless of others. Selah.

35
Who Fixed the Roof?

- part one

—ɯ—

My father died when I was twelve years of age, but God wonderfully provided me with good men who played an important part in the shaping of my life. One such man was Joe Gray, my Bible class teacher. By day he ran a building company, but he also had a great gift of making the Bible stories come alive. Joe profoundly affected the way I continue to view the Bible.

Daniel 11:32 (KJV) says, *"The people that do know their God shall be strong, and do exploits."* Exploits are unusual actions and the key to doing them is the strength that comes from knowing God through his word. I hope you will become stronger as you get to know God better in this Bible story.

When I approach a story in the Bible I try to get to the story behind the story. I work hard to get into the sights, sounds, smells, and emotions involved in it.

The story we are now going to look at concerns the crippled man who was brought by four friends. In their determination to get their friend to Jesus, they broke up the roof of someone's house. You can read it first in Mark 2:1-2 and then in Luke 5:17-26.

The story left me with a strange question: "Who fixed the roof?" The damage would be considerable, so how did the owner feel? It would need to be fixed quickly; after the drama of the miracle when the crowds had all gone home, someone would have to get a tool box out and go up on the roof and fix it.

The reading from Mark informs us that Jesus had returned home to Capernaum. Now we know that Jesus was born in Bethlehem, fled as a refugee with his parents to Egypt and finally settled in Nazareth where he spent his growing up years until he was 30.

But when Jesus began his public ministry, he relocated to Capernaum. This was to fulfil prophecy but it was also a geographically convenient place for his itinerant ministry. It's interesting to think of Jesus living (occasionally) in his home, as a neighbour and part of a local community.

Capernaum was a town that saw an extraordinary amount of miraculous activity (see Mark 1:32-34). It was there that Jairus' daughter, the centurion's servant, and Peter's mother-in-law were all healed. Yet despite this special favour and Jesus' physical presence, the people failed to repent and change their ways (see Matthew 11:23-24). Some suppose that if people see miracles they will quickly turn to God, but Capernaum proved otherwise.

Luke 5:17 gives the backdrop to this healing. As Jesus was teaching the people, religious leaders had come from far and wide to investigate him, so everything he said and did was being observed very critically. Jesus' message and miracles revealed the hollow hypocrisy of the religious authorities, and they could not tolerate that.

But the verse also tells us that, despite such a critical audience, *"The power of the Lord was present for him to heal the sick."* This is a perfect combination – teaching and healing together. There is a saying, "If you have the word without the Spirit you'll dry up, the

Spirit without the word, you'll blow up, but with the word and the Spirit you'll grow up."

Jesus once accused the Sadducees, *"You are in error because you do not know the Scriptures or the power of God"* (Matthew 22:29). For balanced spiritual health we need the word and the Spirit. Read Ezekiel 37 if you want more on this important balance.

So into this atmosphere of teaching about how to live life, and physical healing to restore life, four men arrived, very impatient to get their crippled friend to Jesus.

Four amazing friends

Despite his problems, the paralysed man was blessed with at least four amazing friends. It is important that we appreciate the friends we have but also keep widening our circle, because friends make life. This man's life was changed because of the effort of his friends.

We could learn some lessons from them:

Determination

They were so convinced that Jesus was the answer to their friend's need that no obstacle could stop them. Despite crowds, critical leaders, and even the roof of a house, by all means they would get him to Jesus. Sometimes people need the help of some very determined people to get them through to God.

Faith

Jesus saw this faith when they broke up the roof and stared down into his face below them (he would be covered in dust!). Faith was displayed in those dirty, sweaty, grinning faces that appeared to say, "We've done our bit, but it's over to you now, Jesus." They were united in their faith to get him healed.

Inventiveness

They could have been put off by the size of the crowd, but somehow they got tools and ropes to make an imaginative (and rather destructive) route to Jesus. I am sure there would have been protests at the dust and the mess descending on the pompous leaders below.

We should ask ourselves, "How willing are we to allow our possessions (including our homes) to be available to be 'messed up' to serve the purposes of God?"

36
Who Fixed the Roof?

- part two

—ɯ—

Jesus' teaching must have come to an abrupt stop when a crippled man was lowered down by ropes in front of the Lord from a large hole in the ceiling. Once the dust had settled and the man was lying in front of Jesus, the whole crowd (including the large group of critical clerics) must have wondered what would happen next. Jesus was very impressed by the utter determination of these four men to get their crippled friend to meet him.

The miracle

I wonder if the friends were disappointed at the first words Jesus spoke to the man: *"Cheer up, son your sins are forgiven."* They had come for a miracle, not a confessional!

Characteristically, Jesus gave him what he most needed, rather than what he wanted. He started on the inside and worked his way out to the body. It was the word first, then the power: "Cheer up," and then "Get up." Not all sickness is a result of personal sin, but the Lord was showing that forgiveness of sins is more important even than a miracle of healing for the body. One of the keys to healing is the matter of forgiveness. Jesus obviously knew far more than we do about the needs of this man, and dealt with the greatest need first.

The unbelieving – and unbelievable – religious leaders

The religious police of the day had come from every village in Galilee, Judea and Jerusalem – this wasn't coincidence, this was an organized investigation. It seems as though their minds were made up before they arrived.

Jesus was a challenge to their self-appointed authority, which they were using to control people and for personal financial gain. The confrontation was coming to a head and they were already plotting the death of Jesus (see Mark 3:6). Jesus knew what they were thinking: *"Who is this fellow who speaks blasphemy? Who can forgive sins but God alone?"*

The religious leaders were holding a silent conversation; they had come looking for fault and now they had found it. Jesus put their thoughts onto the loud speaker, asking, *"Why are you thinking these things in your heart?"* They were not angry so much at sins being forgiven, but at the one who was doing the forgiving.

Jesus then demonstrated his authority to forgive by his authority to heal. *"Take up your mat"* wasn't a suggestion, it was a command, and he did. The man immediately got up and began to praise God. I can only imagine what his friends were doing on the roof; I think it would be a very noisy praise party!

People filled with awe and amazement

The man picked up his mat and went walking home with his friends, all praising God. What a day it had been! The crowd also went home filled with amazement and awe at the remarkable things they had seen.

Sadly, the religious leaders went home grinding their teeth in anger at their inability to stop Jesus. What an awful response! The best-trained minds of the day had just seen an amazing miracle but went away angry because Jesus had, once more, rocked their theological boat and challenged their authority.

I wonder what the man did with his mat. I like to think of him hanging it in a prominent place in his home, and when questioned about it, eagerly taking the opportunity to tell of his amazing miracle!

How is your capacity to be amazed?

Mark, the writer of the second gospel, noticed something that others did not – it was Jesus' ability to amaze people. I've counted numerous times in his gospel when he takes note of people's amazed response at Jesus and what he was doing:

"The people were amazed at his teaching...they were completely astonished ... people were overwhelmed with amazement ... the people were overwhelmed with wonder."

We can be amazed at many things – the wonders of our world, computerized graphics, medical science, etc – but have we lost our capacity to be amazed by Jesus? The paralysed man, his friends and the crowd were overwhelmed with amazement at Jesus but the religious leaders, seeing the same event, were filled with angry and murderous thoughts. Angry or amazed, the condition of our heart very much affects what our eyes see.

Who fixed the roof?

As the crowds were wending their way home talking of the amazing miracle, and as the man and his friends for the first time walked home together, someone was getting a tool box out and climbing up on the roof to do some emergency repairs.

Was it one of the grateful friends of the paralysed man? Was it Peter who also lived in Capernaum? He was a fisherman, though. Or was it a time-served carpenter who had been taught his skills in his

Joseph's workshop in Nazareth? Someone fixed the roof because in the middle of the miraculous the mundane tasks still have to go on.

A hymn comes to mind: "I stand amazed in the presence of Jesus..."

37

Get Fit

- part one

—⟨M⟩—

We should have two questions in mind when approaching Scripture or preparing a sermon. What is the truth to be learned? What difference should that truth make in a person's life?

The message and objective in this chapter is simple: to help you get more spiritually fit. The Christian church in the West is suffering from an epidemic of spiritual flabbiness and obesity.

In Jeremiah chapter 12, the prophet was having a serious pity party – *"You are always righteous ... yet I would speak with you about your justice."* He knew that God was always right, but from Jeremiah's point of view, he was not always fair.

God then spoke to the prophet to tell him that things were actually going to get tougher, and so he would need to get fitter. The Lord challenged Jeremiah, *"How will you do in the floods?"* Would he overcome or would he be overcome?

Spiritual flabbiness has a nasty habit of revealing itself at crucial moments. When we consider that the Church is moving towards the climax of history, this is not a good time to be declared "unfit for the task." The final days of the Church will be its most exciting and the most demanding.

In this chapter we are going to look at one of the most colourful and courageous characters in the Bible. God took him on a three-and-a-half year journey of rigorous preparation to make him fit for the biggest challenge of his life. I hope you will find it helpful as you face your own life challenges.

Elijah from Tishbe is this person, who suddenly appears in 1 Kings 17. His first assignment from God was a short and straight message to be delivered to the king – *"There will be neither dew nor rain in the next few years except at my word."*

Then Elijah was commanded by God to go and hide himself in a ravine where he would be fed by ravens and would drink from a brook. So he went missing for the next few years, little knowing that those years of hiding would be the preparation for his next, much bigger, assignment.

There are seasons of busyness in our lives but there are also quieter times which can be part of God's preparation for an upcoming challenge. A major change of season happened in 1998 when I received a phone call from my wife. She had gone down to Bristol to look after our daughter Lorraine who had recently returned home in a very emaciated state from Bangladesh.

We thought Lorraine had contracted an infection while working as a nurse, but that morning the real truth came out – our daughter was a heroin addict. So we began to walk with our daughter through the nightmare world of addiction. We had enjoyed walking with God in the good times of our lives, and now we were to harvest the benefits of this walk as we entered a time of severe challenge.

From 1 Kings we learn that Elijah was a very courageous man but that he also experienced times of fear, paranoia and depression. He even resigned from the ministry thinking he was a failure and asked that God would kill him. All of this because of one threat from a woman, Queen Jezebel! His departure to heaven was quite spectacular (taken up in a chariot of fire), making him one of only two men in the Bible who never passed through death, the other man being Enoch.

Later we will look at some of the crucial lessons God taught him in the 3 ½ hidden years but before we do that I want to skip forward to see what God was preparing him for:

Elijah's challenge ahead

Keep in mind that although Elijah didn't know what was coming, God knew the challenge that was before him, and the preparation that would be necessary.

The contest by fire on Mount Carmel was ahead of him, where he would stand alone against the massed ranks of pagan idolatry. You will find the story in 1 Kings 18:16-46. The God who answered by sending fire on the sacrifice would prove himself as the true God, and the whole nation would be there to witness it. This was going to be big, very big.

God knew that the shaping of 3 ½ years in obscurity would provide the character and faith-building lessons necessary for his forthcoming challenge. God knows what lies ahead for every one of us and in his mercy allows events to come so that we will be *"thoroughly equipped for every good work"* (2 Timothy 3:16-17).

Elijah's season of preparation

God took this man on a journey of preparation during an incredibly difficult time personally and nationally. It was dangerous to be a prophet of God because Ahab was the king, and sitting beside him on the throne was Jezebel, perhaps the most evil woman who has ever lived. Look at 1 Kings 16:25-26, 29-33 for a description of Ahab and his father Omri before him.

The climate of the nation could be described in three words – wickedness, deception and persecution. Queen Jezebel had deceived the whole nation into worshipping Baal with the sacrifice of children. The 450 priests of Baal were the butchers who delivered those sacrifices. To maintain her grip, Jezebel had initiated the persecution and execution of all who worshipped the true God (see 1 Kings 18:4, 13).

It is hard to believe that a nation with such a rich heritage of worship and godly leadership could sink so low into the darkness of pagan idolatry. So in the midst of this hostile climate, God took one of his servants aside for rigorous training.

38
Get Fit

- part two

—⟋⟍—

We are staying with the story of Elijah for a little bit longer to look at the lessons he needed to learn in his season of obscurity – lessons that were needed to make him fit for the major challenge he was about to face.

He learned the need for obedience and courage

"The word of the Lord came to Elijah" is a phrase that crops up a lot. Elijah was a man who listened for the voice of God, and when God spoke he obeyed. That obedience required courage.

Too many Christians today want comfort, blessing, safety, pleasant meetings and anything that makes them feel happy. If they get involved in missions, they prefer short-term ones with accommodation in a hotel, please.

Jim Elliot said, "If Jesus Christ be God and gave himself for me, then no sacrifice that I make is too great for him." This young man and his family and companions made missions their chosen career and literally gave their lives for Christ and the Auca Indians. Where is that spirit today?

Elijah obeyed God's command to go before Ahab, to disappear to Cherith, to move on to Zarephath and finally to climb up Mount Carmel. Hearing God starts with wanting to hear God and then being willing to obey what he says, no matter how big, small, seemingly insignificant or difficult the command.

He learned that waiting is as important to God as working

The nation was in spiritual crisis and it needed a word from God. Yet God told the prophet Elijah to go and hide himself for 3 ½ years of apparent inactivity. It didn't seem logical, but he obeyed.

We are so activity conscious! Many of us have the syndrome of indispensability: the idea that God's work cannot survive without our input. Sadly, we measure a person's worth by what they are doing, whereas to God, "obeying is better than sacrifice." What we think is inactivity can be God's special preparation.

Look at Jesus, living for 90% of his life on earth in the obscurity of a "sink estate" called Nazareth. Think of John the Baptist living in isolation in a desert for 30 years, or Moses toiling as a shepherd for 40 years in the wilderness. Joseph came to full readiness to be Prime Minister after 15 years in an Egyptian prison, while Paul was deprogrammed and re-taught in the quietness of an Arabia desert.

Sometimes the greater the task, the longer the preparation, and we humans often don't handle obscurity and inactivity very well. But Elijah was serving God as much in the loneliness beside the brook Cherith, or in the home of a widow as he was on Mount Carmel. It might not have been easy for him to sit day after day by the brook waiting for the black-coated waiters to fly in with breakfast and dinner, but there was no moving on until God said so.

He learned that humility is essential to service

The command to move on did eventually come after the ravens stopped delivering and the brook stopped flowing. This next lesson for Elijah would, if anything, be harder than the previous ones. For a start he was commanded to go to Zarephath which was right in the middle of Jezebel country.

God was literally preparing a table for him in the presence of his enemies. It would not have been an easy place for a prophet of God, especially as the instrument of provision was a widowed Gentile woman. For a law-abiding, God-fearing Jewish man, this would be a humbling experience. In addition, the widow did not appear to even have enough for her own needs, far less for a fugitive prophet as well.

Even in the midst of hostile Jezebel territory, God had a woman who was willing to obey him. It is true that often in the most unlikely places God has placed amazing people. Elijah had to accept help from a most unlikely person but being humbled like this was an important part of his preparation. The Apostle Paul had a physical disability that meant he needed the help of carers to enable him to fulfil his ministry, which must have challenged the independent spirit of a previously self-assured and self-reliant Pharisee.

Humility is contrary to the flesh and certainly runs counter to the prevailing spirit of our generation. Yet walking in humility is part of following our Saviour who "humbled himself and became obedient to death, even death on a cross." Satan humiliates to destroy us but God humbles us to develop us.

He learned the importance of total dependence on God

Elijah was going to face the combined demonic power of Baal and Asherah (850 prophets in total) alone. There wouldn't be the remotest chance of him faking a victory – if no fire came, he would be totally exposed. His dependence on God was total.

But at Cherith and Zarephath he had learned that God could be totally relied upon for supply. His life had been stripped of pride and he had developed a prompt obedience to God that would not question even when commanded to do something illogical like dousing the sacrifice three times with water.

Elijah was as willing to "go and hide himself" as he was when God finally said, "go show yourself." Many of us prefer the "go show" to the "go hide"! Philip the Evangelist was similarly obedient when God commanded to him to leave the multitudes in the revival in Samaria and head for the desert where one man needed someone to explain scripture to him. That man happened to be the Chancellor of the Exchequer for Queen Candace of Ethiopia.

We are very fond of quick solutions and a relatively easy course of preparation with plenty of humour thrown in and a few easy steps to success. The ministry of Elijah was spectacular but it followed serious preparation in a man who despite his failings was willing to submit to God's school of discipline. We too have a part to play in maintaining our spiritual fitness so that we can be ready to make a difference.

39
From Sunset to Sunrise

- part one

—⟋⟍—

The story we are going to look at is regarded as one of the most moving dramas in the Bible. It opens with despair and closes with joy.

Luke 24 is one of those "hinge" chapters in the Bible, because so much turns on its outcome. The cross had shattered the lives of the disciples but the resurrection completely changed their future. The forty days before the ascension was an important time of personal and group encounters with the Lord, and Luke 24:13-35 records such an encounter for two disciples.

The amazing Christ
Jesus had just accomplished the most important event in history, something planned before the world was made, an event that has repercussions for all of creation. Through the cross and the resurrection:

- Christ had scored the greatest victory over Satan, the arch-enemy of mankind
- His blood opened the way for people to approach God in righteousness
- The first fruits of the resurrection had been seen in Jerusalem with previously dead people appearing in the city (See Matthew 27:51-53)
- An earthquake had ripped the temple curtain from top to bottom

And in the midst of these immense events, Jesus took the time to go for an unhurried walk with two very disillusioned disciples. What a truly amazing Christ, who will go to extraordinary lengths to help hurting saints!

Two hurting disciples

It's not hard to see the evidence of emotional distress in these two disciples. The last few years had been nothing short of amazing as they followed Jesus – the sermons, the miracles, the crowds. The whole nation had been rocked to its foundation and expectations of liberation from the Romans were very high. But the events of the last few days had shattered all this – Jesus was dead and it seemed that the determined religious authorities had finally won.

For these two disciples, the stranger who drew alongside them and matched his pace with theirs seemed to be so out of touch with recent events. Yet I love the phrase, *"Jesus himself came up and walked along with them."* His care for them was so personal and his questions opened the gates of grief in their hearts so that all the pent-up disappointment came pouring out.

Their words must have come out with a hint of exasperation and impatience – *"Are you only a visitor to Jerusalem and do not know the things that have happened there in these days?"* Then the distraught condition of their hearts is shown – *"We had hoped that he was the one who was going to redeem Israel."* These words reveal the real pain and shattered hope.

The downcast faces finished off the picture of two disciples in total despair who had very quickly plummeted from the height of expectancy to the depth of hopelessness – "Why had God allowed this to happen to his own Son?"

Handling disappointment is a very hard thing, when people, career, health, marriage or friendships fail to fulfil expectations. But the hardest of all is when it appears that God himself has let you down. Perhaps it can seem that all the miracles and answers are happening to other people. With your head you know that God doesn't have favourites and that he loves all his family, but it doesn't feel that way in your heart.

This then was the very sad human scenario that Jesus met as he walked the familiar road from Jerusalem to Emmaus with Cleopas and his companion. You may be familiar with the verse from Proverbs 13:12, *"Hope deferred makes the heart grow sick."* The Message puts it like this – *"Unrelenting disappointment leaves you heartsick,"* concluding, *"but a sudden good break can turn life around."*

For these two disciples, that "sudden break" came in the person of a walking companion on their journey to Emmaus. But Jesus did not come just to question and sympathise, he came to bring wonderful change. He began in the simplest of ways – he asked pertinent questions and allowed them to answer.

There are very few really good listeners, people who are not trotting out a clichéd answer before the speaker has finished explaining how they feel. The art of listening is a rare one, because so many want to be heard rather than listen. Steve Covey in his book, *The Seven Habits of Highly Effective People*, said, "Seek first to understand then to be understood." To give a person your time is to give them a precious gift – focussed listening in a way that endeavours to understand the hurting heart behind the words.

The beginning of the transformation

After the two disciples had vented their feelings, it was time for

Jesus to give them the best Bible study of their lives, which will be the theme of the next chapter.

40

From Sunset to Sunrise

- part two

—⟋⟍—

Emmaus lies west of Jerusalem, so as the two disciples were making their way to the village they were walking into the sunset. Later, as the day was nearly over, they invited Jesus into their home. But after an illuminating Bible study with Jesus they were so excited that they got up and headed back to Jerusalem, then walking into the sunrise. What a change from sunset to sunrise for these two disciples!

At the sunset stage of their journey they were going through the trauma of shattered hope. They were heartsick with disappointment; their dream had become a nightmare. Little did they realise that they were on edge of a breakthrough that would turn their lives around (and their direction). What they thought was the end really was the beginning.

For us to experience the same change there are two truths we need to keep in mind:

1.God's ways are far higher than ours.

We tend to just be concerned with the immediate situation whereas God is working to a long-term timetable. We often misunderstand God because we try to fit his eternal ways into our time-controlled ways.

2.God's purpose for us is far greater than we realise.

We are very concerned about our comfort, safety and prosperity, whereas he is more concerned about our character development. We want easy options, instant answers and quick deliverance, but God wants robust and mature believers who can handle adversity and global challenge.

How Jesus brought about their transformation

After he got them revealing the real issues of their hearts, Jesus then began to give them new revelation, especially about himself in all of the Scripture. He also gave them a new insight into suffering – that it was part of God's purpose and process for the fulfilling of his plan. We naturally avoid suffering, but there will be no advance to maturity without it and no progress to the fulfilling of God's long-term plan without his people being willing to pay this price.

In Romans 5:3, Paul makes a humanly illogical statement: *"We rejoice in our sufferings..."* These verses are well worth reading to see what suffering (and suffering alone) produces. Jesus had to go through suffering to enter his glory and we, his servants, have not been given a special route to glory that avoids it.

Jesus put new heart into them, changing them from broken hearts to burning hearts. The disciples were beginning to realise that this was not the end but a glorious new beginning. The whole agenda was changed; before, they were selfishly nationalistic in their desires, but now he was lifting their vision to taking his kingdom to the whole world.

These disciples thought they knew the scriptures, but Jesus

opened up a whole new panorama of understanding with a broader concept of God's purpose. They thought they had known Jesus, but after his death and resurrection he kept appearing and disappearing, as he was no longer restricted to the limitations of a human body. The truth was slowly dawning that he was the omnipresent Christ for every disciple in every place.

No wonder their hearts were burning inside them! Their future was not in their past; this was not about recapturing the glory days from Jesus' previous time with them. Their future was the dawning of a new day. We learn from the past but we cannot live in it.

When these two disciples got back to Jerusalem, they met up with the other disciples who had similar stories of life-transforming encounters with the risen Christ. It is only the resurrected Christ who can turn sunsets in sunrises.